Talent and Tenacity

Dr Lachlan Grant of Ballachulish
His Life and Times

Dr Lachlan Grant

Talent and Tenacity

Dr Lachlan Grant of Ballachulish

His Life and Times

RODERICK MACLEOD

To
Mrs Sheena Roddan
and in memory of her late sisters
Dr Marie and Miss Eleanora Grant

British Library Cataloguing in Publication Data
A catalogue record of this book is available from the British Library

ISBN 978-1-904817-11-6

Typeset by XL Publishing Services, Exmouth
Printed in Great Britain by SRP Ltd, Exeter
for House of Lochar
Isle of Colonsay, Argyll PA61 7YR

Contents

Foreword

PROFESSOR JAMES HUNTER CBE, FRSE, PHD

In the summer of 2013, as this book was being finalised, NHS Highland made it known that – following their failure to find doctors willing to deliver primary health care to people on Canna, Eigg, Muck, Rum and in adjacent mainland localities – it might be necessary to offer prospective recruits substantial 'golden hellos', or starting bonuses, on top of initial salaries of £75,000. It is understandable that general practitioners accustomed to five-day weeks and to regular (as well as regulated) hours might find it challenging to work in places where they could be called on to deal single-handedly and at all hours with medical emergencies. But it is equally the case that NHS Highland's recruitment difficulties serve to highlight the remarkable dedication of earlier generations of medical practitioners who – for financial rewards a lot less generous than those available today – were prepared to spend much, or all, of their working lives in rural and remote communities where, night or day, weekend or weekday, they were expected to be always available.

One such community is the West Highland village of Ballachulish. Together with its extensive hinterland, Ballachulish – in a way that is certainly exceptional and possibly unique – was, for a period of 103 years, served successively by three medical men who, between them, spanned the entire twentieth century. They were Dr Lachlan Grant (45 years Ballachulish's GP), Dr William MacKenzie (32 years) and Dr Roderick Macleod (26 years). Now the last of the three, Roderick Macleod, has researched and written this account of, and tribute to, the life and work of the first, Lachlan Grant. For Macleod this has been something of a labour of love – one fuelled by his conviction that Grant is deserving of remembrance in Ballachulish, in the Highlands and in Scotland more generally.

Macleod is right to feel this. As someone who grew up in the vicinity of Ballachulish and who went on to have an involvement with both Highland history and Highland development, I ought to have been well aware for many years of Lachlan Grant and his many contributions to Highland betterment. But I was not. Inexcusably, Grant's thinking, his writings, his political and cultural campaigning – all of which attracted a great deal of media and other attention during his lifetime – were permitted, after Grant's death in 1945, to fade almost entirely from view. Until very recently, therefore, all I knew of Lachlan Grant was that, as far back as the early 1930s, he advocated a comprehensive Highland development strategy of a sort eventually brought partly – but only partly – to fruition with the formation in 1964 of the Highlands and Islands Development Board (since reconstituted as Highlands and Islands Enterprise).

That I now know a lot more about Lachlan Grant is due to Roderick Macleod and to the growing academic interest in Grant that his researches have helped stimulate and inform. As following pages demonstrate, Grant was a man who could have had a glittering career elsewhere but who, turning his back on that career, chose to spend his life in the Highlands. Lachlan Grant, however, was in no way looking to have things easy. Rather the reverse. As Roderick Macleod shows, Grant's years as Ballachulish's doctor, between 1900 and 1945, were years during which this extraordinarily talented and hard-working individual strove successfully to make his mark in a whole multitude of fields. He kept abreast of, and in fact contributed to, medical advances. He became central to a Ballachulish labour dispute of nationwide significance. He was a leading advocate of the creation in 1913 of a Highlands and Islands precursor of the later National Health Service. He pressed for Highland land reform and Highland industrialisation. He took a close interest in Gaelic revivalism and shinty. He knew personally, and was in close contact with, nationally eminent politicians like Ramsay Macdonald and Tom Johnston.

For much of the nineteenth and twentieth centuries, the Highlands – for reasons bound up with underdevelopment of the kind Lachlan Grant sought to combat – were an area which people of ability mostly left forever on completing their education. Grant was one of very few individuals to break with this pattern and, indeed, to do what he could to create circumstances intended to reverse depopulation by making the Highlands the prosperous, economically dynamic place that Lachlan Grant believed so passionately the Highlands could and ought to be. Grant merits our admiration. And Roderick Macleod, whose book so strongly makes that point, deserves our thanks.

James Hunter, September 2013

Acknowledgements

I am grateful to Mrs Sheena Roddan, Dr Grant's sole surviving daughter, for granting permission to publish this biographical account, the life and times of her late father. Mrs Roddan, her daughter Susan, and the Grant family in its wider circle have all been a huge help in providing access to all material relevant and essential to make the project interesting, informative and revealing. They are rightly proud of their family roots: Dr Lachlan Grant was an inspiration to everyone. I was very privileged to be given access to Dr Grant's journals, papers and publications, for one year prior to them being deposited in the National Library of Scotland. This facilitated a full detailed scrutiny, in the comfort of Craigleven, of what is core material to an account of his life. In the same vein, Mrs Rae Grant, widow of Hugh Grant, nephew of Dr Grant, has been generous of her time and support to this project. She kindly furnished me with a chest stuffed full of family papers, and documents of personal business and legal relevance: a treasure trove in itself. I would also wish to recognise the contribution of her daughter, Mrs Morag Watt, in providing detailed family information. Similarly, Mr John Grant, a great-nephew of Dr Grant, has assisted immeasurably on family detail and data. On the Clark family side, I have to relate, no one could be more supportive to me than Mr Duncan Clark, the son of Angus Clark, and nephew-in-law of Dr Grant. Duncan is a lawyer, and the accuracy of the mountain of material he provided is both impressive and laudable. In much the same mode, his retired GP cousin, Dr Iain Clark, readily gave unstinting help in furnishing me with meticulous detail relating to Grant's education through school, college and Edinburgh University Medical School, and the awards he gained pre- and post-graduation.

Outwith the Grant and Clark families, the contribution of my old friend from Golspie, Dr Michael Simpson, is worth recording. Dr Michael is one in a long line of Simpsons, a medical dynasty that has well served the county of Sutherland for generations, and to give me access to and copies of the relevant papers and letters of Dr James B Simpson, is to me a great prize. Dr J.B.S was GP in Ballachulish 1889-1892, and knew Grant as a boy, as doctor and friend. In 1945, Dr Simpson wrote the Dr Grant obituary for the *BMJ*.

Other GP colleagues who have supported the project and provided good material on which to build are Dr Chris Robinson and Dr James Douglas of Fort William. Both doctors contributed constructively on the health services, and the Dewar Committee in particular, significant as it was in Dr Grant's own time and close to his heart.

Access to local school registers and log books was afforded to me by Mr Sam Clark, headmaster of Ballachulish Primary School. I sincerely thank him for his readiness in this matter. Likewise, insight and information into Voluntary and NHS Hospitals as provided by Mr Jim Leslie, is a debt I readily acknowledge. Mr Colin Waller and Ms Anne Macleod of Highland Archive Services in Inverness and Skye have been a valuable pair of contributors on factual and photographic material. Alex Gillespie of Corpach has also ably assisted on the photographic side, and I thank him sincerely.

Not surprisingly, ferreting and sourcing information as provided through National Census, Registers of Births, Deaths and Marriages, is a nightmare. Testing of the same for accuracy and consistency is more so. In this context I found the patience and persistence of Ms Christine MacKay of Luing absolutely invaluable, and I am deeply grateful to her for such input. Staff at the National Library of Scotland in Edinburgh, staff at the public library in Fort William, and staff at the *Oban Times* offices have all been singularly helpful and accommodating. I thank them all.

To my brother 'RJ' and his wife Lorna, whose hospitality-without-bounds I enjoyed on my many missions to the National Library of Scotland in Edinburgh, I extend special thanks; it did mean that part of the exercise, at least, was not a hardship. Moreover, I thank Lorna for her diligence in proof-reading all written material prior to its delivery to the publishers.

If patience be a virtue or be personified, then such an honour rests comfortably with my wife Maggie, who has been ever steadfast and sure throughout.

For Kevin Byrne and his staff at the House of Lochar, I reserve a sincere thanks for the important task of publication, so professionally attended to and performed. In particular, I am greatly indebted to Dilly Emslie (Lady Kingarth) for elegantly editing the original manuscript, and to Lucy Emslie for her efficient transcription of the text to electronic version. Big tasks, well done. I am most grateful.

Finally, may I thank a quartet of academics whose specialist input and support one cannot fail to recognise, and they are:

Prof. James Hunter, Emeritus Professor of History at the Highlands and Islands University, for his Foreword to the book and much support along the way.

Prof. Ewan Cameron, Professor of History at Edinburgh University, for much advice, support, and guidance towards publication.

Prof. Neville Kirk, formerly of Manchester University, for generous exchange of information and material relating to Ballachulish Slate Quarries, the slate industry, and the 'Lock Out' issues. Prof Kirk's own book *Custom and Conflict in the 'Land of the Gael'* is a valuable, well-researched work of reference.

Dr Annie Tindley, Lecturer in Social History at Glasgow Caledonian University, for her strenuous efforts to gain national educational coverage of Dr Grant as a medical pioneer and social reformer.

Roderick Macleod

1

The Early Years

Johnstone in Renfrewshire was the birthplace of Dr Lachlan Grant, and the place where he spent the first nine years of his life. The town lies three miles west of Paisley and some twelve miles west of the city of Glasgow. It was founded in 1781 on the site of Brig o' Johnstone, then only a hamlet of ten people. In 1782, the local laird, George Ludovic Houston, commissioned designs for a town, consisting of a series of regular residential streets with two civic squares, one at each end, and a parish church, which was completed later in 1794. This planned town grew up around Johnstone Castle, then the seat of the Houston family, and it grew pretty rapidly. In the early stages the town population was around 1,500 and by 1831 its resident population had risen to near the 5,600 mark. Steady industrial development was making an impact. Local industry brought coal mining, thread-making and cotton weaving to the town, causing its considerable and rapid growth in size. Indeed by 1871, the year Lachlan Grant was born, the population of Johnstone had climbed to over 7,000 souls. Of the industries that set up in the town, the main established industry was related to the thread and cotton trade with mills readily powered by the Black Cart Water, a river which runs its course to the north of Johnstone town itself. From early on, engineering works also prospered in the town. On account of such dynamism Johnstone became known as the 'engineering burgh.' In fact, the burgh laid claim to have started up the first firm in Britain for the manufacture of machine tools, which was founded in 1815.

Lachlan Grant was born on 18 April 1871 in Johnstone. His father and mother were both natives of the Renfrewshire town and Lachlan's other siblings, those born before 1880, were also born there. His paternal grandfather, however, who was also called Lachlan, came from the Dingwall area of Ross-shire. Young Lachlan was named after the grandfather in the true Highland tradition. This direct link to the Highlands of Scotland was ultimately to play a pivotal part in Dr Grant's own life and his aspirations. It most likely proved to be decisive in the many roles he played, and fulfilled, in later years.

Grandfather Lachlan migrated south from his native Ross-shire while still a young active man and a bachelor. He was a fully trained craftsman, a joiner and carpenter, and equipped with these skills arrived in Johnstone in search of gainful employment. By trade, as noted, this was in carpentry. Yet according to one set of census returns, he spent some time, at least, as a 'cotton spinner.' The records, however, suggest he enjoyed regular paid employment throughout his working lifetime in the town. In 1822, Lachlan (senior) was to marry a local Johnstone lady by the name of Miss Isabella Stewart. Following marriage they set up home at 14 Collier Street, a central part of the town itself. They settled there and went on to rear a family of four children: Ann, Margaret, Isabella and their youngest one, Peter. The family were close-knit and supportive of one another, and soon merged to be an integral part of the Renfrewshire community. In the years ahead they were all, as individuals and as a family, to contribute greatly to the local society and its economy.

Though Isabella, the mother, died at a relatively young age, leaving husband Lachlan with the four children, the surviving family were to hold firmly together and continue to live at 14 Collier Street, until such later time as they themselves set to marry and/or establish homes of their own. Lachlan Grant (senior) died in 1864 at the age of 81 years.

From that nexus it is through the life and person of Peter Grant and his descendants that the 'Dr Grant story' really rolls out and unfolds. On attaining school-leaving age, the young Peter Grant trained by way of serving an apprenticeship as a cartwright. The census returns of the time record this particular fact. However, he was also to train as a joiner and cabinet-maker, and subsequently to establish a business of this kind. By all accounts Peter Grant was a fit, handsome man. He was also an enterprising individual with a strong work ethic, who firmly upheld the importance of earning a living and maintaining a family life of the best possible quality. It was no doubt with such aim that, along with his good friend and colleague Archibald McFarlane, he set up and operated the firm they named Grant & McFarlane. This firm traded as cabinet-makers, engineers, wood merchants, joiners and saw-millers and was based, as their advertisements proclaimed, at 'The Works, and at The Saw Mills in Johnstone, near Glasgow.' The business traded well and actively, serving not just the town itself but also the wider west of Scotland area. To all concerned, it seemed Peter Grant was an outstanding example of success. This sense of prosperity was to extend well beyond his business affairs to his social life and his status, when it became public knowledge that he had won the hand and heart of one of the most eligible young ladies in Renfrewshire, Miss Jean Paton of Johnstone. On 30 June 1870 Peter Grant tied the knot with Jean Paton at a marriage ceremony held at her home, Cartbank, in the town. Jean was the eldest of the three daughters of Mr and Mrs William Paton of Paton Mills Ltd., then the dominant manufacturer of boot and shoe laces in the world, producing

25 million pairs of laces annually. At the height of the Industrial Revolution, Patons Ltd. was founded in Johnstone in 1840 by William Paton: himself, then a 21-year-old local man and entrepreneur of note. The Paton dynasty was to run on for some 150 years until 1990, when the firm was bought over by an Irish manufacturing company. There is no doubting the fact that Peter Grant married into a family of real wealth and worth. Fortunately, the Grant/Paton union was based on much more than material values; it rested firmly on the sure foundation of the Christian faith, as evidenced and reflected in all the private and personal letters handwritten by them, and exchanged in the years and months prior to marriage. Clearly they were both spiritually aware and committed people, possibly even evangelical in outlook. They were evidently well suited too, and comfortable in their newly-linked lives.

In 1871 Peter and Jean Grant were blessed with their child, a boy, whom they christened Lachlan, after his paternal grandfather. As the years rolled on the family was to expand to five boys and two girls in all. There were two other male children born to them, who died in infancy. On every front otherwise, life was seen to bestow many bounties and blessings upon them. Family life was as sound and secure as one could realistically wish for and the business itself was thriving and prosperous. Confidence rested at such a level that by 3 November 1876 Peter Grant proposed the sole take-over of the jointly-run business, Grant & McFarlane; this was with the mutual consent of Mr Archibald McFarlane his colleague and hitherto active business partner.

Alas, many tragic events in one's life unfold when least expected or foreseen, only to strike at the very heart of one's existence. Thus it proved to be in the case of Peter and Jean Grant in 1878, when out of a clear blue sky there struck the City of Glasgow Bank scandal. Countless well-established and successful businesses operating in Glasgow, and the west of Scotland region particularly, were bludgeoned into a state of bankruptcy by this catastrophic event. The demise of the City of Glasgow Bank, with fraudulent activity allegedly at its heart, had a cataclysmic effect on innumerable individuals. The tragedy engulfed Peter Grant and, like many businessmen of his ilk, he was reduced to penury. His business went to the wall. The family livelihood had vanished in the blink of an eye. It was a bleak and dark time from all angles and on all fronts. A future in Johnstone had ebbed away. The family's conclusion was that life had to be reframed, that their future had to be carved out elsewhere and certainly in some new direction. The big question was, where next?

Invariably, adversity always puts one to greater test. At such a crippling time as this for the Grant family, the true worth of family values, of unity and solidarity could not have been better tried nor tested. Neither could the fair face of Fortune have smiled so kindly and unexpectedly upon them. For to the

1 Peter Grant, Lachlan Grant's father

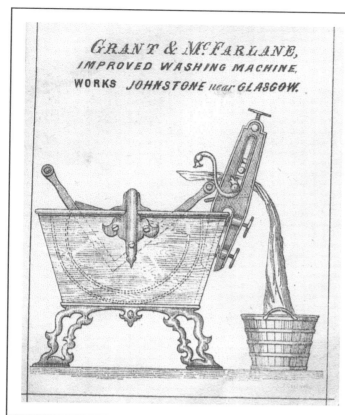

2
Grant & McFarlane advertising their wares – 'Improved Washing Machine'

rescue scene rode a family member in the shape and form of Peter Grant's eldest sister, Annie Barr.

Mrs Barr had been in business in Renfrewshire on her own account, as a grocer, when she was single. Late on in life she married Mr Peter Barr, then a widower, who was himself a grocer. Together they had run grocery shops in both towns of Johnstone and Kilbarchan. Annie Barr had subsequently become widowed and felt as much a need as a desire to carve a new life for herself away from the current woes and, better still, set base in some 'new' community. In Mrs Barr's situation, and importantly on a financial level, she had amassed significant personal wealth and her assets remained intact.

From early leisure travels and holidays in the North and West Highlands she had often cherished a desire to live somewhere in the Glencoe area. Clearly, it did not take her long to decide. By early 1880 she had moved, lock, stock and barrel, north to Ballachulish and Glencoe. Quite opportunely she persuaded her brother Peter, his wife Jean, and their young family, to migrate with her. In Ballachulish village she bought the lease on the Stores Building, and straightaway she established her own new business, to trade in the name,

'Barr & Coy., General Grocers, Drapery and Ironmongery Stores, Ballachulish, Glencoe.' Thus it could truly be said that Ann Barr was back in business, one she knew like the back of her hand.

To assist her, Ann Barr engaged her brother Peter and his wife Jean to be store managers. (They took over the running of the firm on their own account, following the death of Ann Barr on 9 May 1893.) The family move, and their installation at Ballachulish, must have proved a good deal easier and a lot more convenient than expected. For above the ground floor shopping area, the building provided a generous and very spacious flat on the first floor and second floors, which could accommodate them all as one united family. Barr's Stores, Loanfern, was set to be their new place of work, the new family home, and the prospect of future success.

As it happened, this period in the life of the Ballachulish/Glencoe community was a relatively settled one. A new 15 year lease of the slate quarries had just been signed over to Dr D. Campbell, who resided at Craigrannoch, near Ballachulish Ferry. He was a distinguished medical graduate of Edinburgh Medical School but not active in a medical professional capacity at the time, and solely occupied as an active businessman. Locals held him in very good regard and they felt a great deal more confident about employment under his reign over the quarries. It may be noted that, unlike many Highland villages at the time, Ballachulish district at least had its own old-established slate industry in its midst, fickle and market dependent though it be. Nevertheless, like all remote rural areas of the Highlands in those days, it ran closely along the poverty line. Its housing stock especially was singled out as being of major concern in political, social and medical circles, so poor were living conditions, and so lacking the basic amenities. Overcrowding was one serious issue. On the positive side it was, however, a stable and tightly-knit community, of strong Gaelic culture and, by tradition, deeply rooted in the Christian faith. This was the character of the community into whose bosom the 'immigrant' Grants were to be warmly welcomed in 1880. The local people, moreover, had confidence in the village food-store being in the hands of independent and impartial operators and not in the ownership of the estate or the quarry-masters.

Annie Barr, Peter and Jean Grant felt very comfortable in their new setting, and pleased with the reception they received throughout the district. The trauma and turmoil of recent times was now an experience placed in the past and they felt confident about the future for a young and growing family. Besides, restoring and stabilising the family finances mattered to Peter and Jean Grant, who also had to review their children's early education and give it necessary consideration. They were convinced of the need to give the children a stable upbringing and the best possible education to foster independence, for

3 Home Deliveries – Ready to load

4 Early Days : Barr's Stores, Ballachulish

the sake of their future success. To the Grant family, the terror of the 1878 bank collapse was salutary and formed for them one of life's biggest lessons: never to be forgotten and, hopefully, never to be repeated.

When the family moved north in 1880 Lachlan Grant, the eldest of the young family, was a mere nine or ten years of age. He had commenced primary education in the local public school in Johnstone, and continued there until the family's uprooting and move north. Primary schooling was resumed at Ballachulish Public School; he and his brother William both enrolled on the same day, 26 April 1880. From his early schooldays it became evident Lachlan was a very gifted child with high intelligence, and a quick and creative mind. He was picked out by the headmaster, Mr McKerchar, for some special attention. Mr McKerchar was held in high regard as a teacher and renowned as a scholar. He stimulated the young lad mentally and gave him every bit of encouragement to advance his education. Life as a country boy, however, had to be about much more than schoolwork and homework and by all accounts Lachlan was an active boy, physical in his leisure and sporting abilities. His boyhood companion in and around the village was a local lad by the name of Alex Connell, who later in life became minister of Regent Street Presbyterian Church in Glasgow. As boys they spent their free days on nature rambles, climbing on the slopes of Sgurr Dearg and exploring the corries among the surrounding hills and bens. On leaving the local school at the age of fourteen years, Lachlan Grant took up temporary work as a clerk in the quarry offices of Dr Campbell, the leaseholder of the Ballachulish Slate Quarries. While employed in this role he was involved in bookkeeping, in communication activity, and 'in matters of correspondence', and he perfected these skills over his course of time there. The period he spent in the quarry offices was, essentially, a 'Gap' experience, and a sure means of earning some money towards his future, pending, tuition fees. Lachlan was indeed to advance his studies and under the tutelage of the Rev Duncan MacMurchy, who was an able Classics scholar, he was instructed in both Latin and Greek. This extra coaching paved the way to even further study, this time under a Mr Boag who at the time ran a private College of Education on Great Western Road in Glasgow. The sole aim of the college was to educate students to the level of learning required to gain qualifications necessary for entrance to a Scottish university, and access to the profession of one's choice. As a seventeen-year-old student, Lachlan Grant became well aware of the fact that serious study lay ahead of him.

2

The Talented Student

Lachlan Grant initially sat the Glasgow University preliminary examinations and, on gaining entrance qualification, went on to attend the Arts class there for two sessions or so. At that stage he changed his mind in regard to his studies and decided to switch Faculties from Arts to Medicine, leave Glasgow, and enrol in Edinburgh University. On 2 May 1889 he matriculated at Edinburgh University, having passed his medical prelims earlier that year and gained the necessary entrance qualifications. Before him stretched a full five-year course of study, which he undertook with great diligence and marked success. At entry to medical school he was eighteen years of age. Right through his medical course he shone academically and gained the commendation of all his professors, emerging as an outstanding medical student of his academic year.

On route to graduation he collected several prizes, including the Class Medals in Anatomy and (jointly) Eye Diseases, and the Class Prize in Clinical Surgery. On 17 April 1894, at the relatively young age of twenty-three years, he graduated, gaining an M.B., C.M. (with distinction). While he proceeded with his pre-registration house officer jobs in and around Edinburgh, Grant continued his studies to achieve even more advanced medical qualification, gaining his M.D. (Edin.) (with commendation) in 1896 – the earliest date permitted by the university to do so, namely, two years after the initial medical graduation date.

Between his graduation day and 1896, Dr Grant spent time gainfully acquiring knowledge and extending experience in a variety of other medical disciplines, such as psychiatry and eye diseases. He visited the United States of America and Canada to study and compare American, Canadian and British methods and treatments. In Canada he spent time at the Victoria General Hospital in Montreal, the world-famous medical establishment, which was funded and erected in good measure by Lord Strathcona and his many legacies.

While he was in his final year at medical school, Lachlan Grant, as student and undergraduate, came to the notice of one very special Edinburgh consultant. Having collected the medal in eye diseases, it was no wonder the professor in ophthalmology paid no little attention to him, and took him under his wing. It has always been customary for leading consultants to engage in talent spotting at medical school. In circumstances such as this, Lachlan Grant could not have impressed a more illustrious professional in medical circles than Professor Douglas Moray Cooper Lamb Argyll Robertson, to give him his full name, who was a world authority in the field of eye diseases. A graduate of St Andrews and Berlin universities, Prof. Argyll Robertson's own career and professional reputation reigned high. He was honorary eye physician to Queen Victoria, to King Edward VII and to the Royal Household, as well as to other leading world figures of that era. Dr Grant was invited to assist him at his specialist clinics in and around Edinburgh. There is little doubt, and much evidence to suggest, that the talented young doctor was being discreetly groomed for higher professional goals and towards a glittering future career. In parallel, he also attracted the attention of another consultant of acclaim: the head of psychiatry in Edinburgh, Dr Thomas S. Clouston of the Morningside Asylum. Thomas Smith Clouston, or 'TS' (as he was known), was Orcadian, an Edinburgh M.D. and gold medallist, whose reputation rose to doyen status in his speciality. Dr Grant served his hospital clinics too, and attended his patients. He formed a true and lasting friendship with him.

All in all, given such circumstances, it must have stunned and greatly perplexed his superiors, and the entire Edinburgh medical establishment, when in 1896 Dr Grant declared his intention to leave the city and head north to practise his profession in the remote and rural Highlands of Scotland, accepting the post of assistant medical officer to Dr MacCalman of Oban. While in Argyllshire he submitted his original thesis on the subject of 'Observations on Eye Work,' the opus for which Edinburgh University conferred on him the M.D. (with Hons.) in 1896. In due course of time his services to patients in Oban were on public record as being 'much appreciated.' The early move in 1896 from Oban with promotion to yet another post must, however, have come just a tad too soon for patients' liking. Reality would point to the fact that Dr Lachlan Grant had far further to go professionally, and his career at that moment in time had barely taken off.

When Edinburgh University published its list of final results in July 1893, *The Scotsman* of Saturday 29 July contained the following entries:

DISEASES OF THE EYE

First-Class Honours. – 1, Lachlan Grant, Scotland, and John S. Flett, Kirkwall – equal (Medallists); 3, Robert W. Briggs, Derby; 4, George A. Dickson, Edinburgh; 5, T.R.S. Sibbald, Scotland, and W. Russell Strapp, Natal – equal; 7, Samuel Edgerle, West Africa; 8, W. McD.

Selby, Wigtonshire.

D. ARGYLL ROBERTSON, M.D., Lecturer.
JOHN KIRKPATRICK, Sec. Sen. Acad.

July 1893

MENTAL DISEASES

First-Class Certificate – 1, James Anderson, M.B. (Medallist); 2, R.W. Briggs and Eugene A. Darling – equal; 4, Samuel Edgerley, M.B.; 5, Frank Oliphant; 6, J.M. Menzies and Lachlan Grant – equal; 8, W. Russell Strapp; 9, Reginald St G. Bond; 10, A. Hill Buchan; 11, James M. Rutherford.

T.S. CLOUSTON, M.D., Lecturer.

3

Into Medicine

In the year 1896 as he arrived in Oban, a GP assistant to Dr MacCalman, Dr Lachlan Grant was to surprise his colleagues even more. Spreading his wings wider and further, he headed north to the Isle of Skye to take up post as medical officer to Gesto Hospital in Edinbane. At the time Gesto served the whole island and it was the only location in Skye at which any patient could obtain dispensary and clinic-type care. Gesto itself was an interesting concept of care: the product of a generous endowment bequeathed by Kenneth MacLeod, of Gesto originally and later of Greshornish, who left Skye for India in 1824 aged 15 years, with but a guinea in his pocket, and who returned in the 1840s to his island of birth, the land of his forefathers, a retired indigo planter with a fortune to his name.

Determined to do his level best by his fellow islanders, he gifted Gesto hospital, and funds to sustain it, to the people of Skye. Hospitals like Gesto existed in other parts of the Highlands as well and were known as 'voluntary hospitals.' In every case they existed entirely thanks to legacies from local lairds, estates, or monied benefactors. Examples of such establishments in the North, and their benefactors, are the Belford Hospital at Fort William and the Glenfintaig Estate, the County Hospital in Oban and the Bullough family of Fasnacloich, Leanchoil Hospital in Forres and Lord Strathcona. Vacancies arising at these hospitals tended to attract a vast field of high calibre candidates, the generous salaries on offer ranking amongst the highest fees paid in the medical profession. In regard to the Gesto vacancy of 1896, for example, for which Dr Grant had applied, over sixty medical applicants lined up. Nevertheless, it served to demonstrate the esteem in which he himself was held that he was unanimously appointed to the post at twenty-five years of age. Much in Dr Grant's favour, it was said, was his bilingual status; he was a fluent Gaelic speaker, and a well-rounded Gael of culture, who was also viewed to be progressive in thought and deed.

Undoubtedly, Gesto was an onerous responsibility and prevailing conditions on the island at the time were nothing short of distressing. Some notable former MO incumbents of the post were Dr Keith N. MacDonald, the

5 Portrait of Kenneth Macleod of Greshornish

compiler of the well-known 'Gesto Collection of Highland Music,' and grandson-in-law of Neil Macleod of Gesto, and Dr Roger MacNeill, who hailed from the Isle of Colonsay. Prior to Dr MacDonald, the appointment was held by Dr MacNeill, who in 1890 was to become the first MOH to be appointed in Argyllshire. Dr Roger MacNeill was one of the most respected medical figures of his day and the quality of his public health work became a benchmark for medical men to aspire to. In his turn, Dr Lachlan Grant was to prove an equally redoubtable figure: reliable, resilient, and not one to let the side or his profession down.

The appointment was in every way the antithesis of his Edinburgh experience. Serving single-handedly, without peers to share the problems or the workload, it was inevitably lonely. Rural, remote and inaccessible, it could take days to get to and from one's patients. Absence of service networks, medications and equipment made many missions impossible. Whilst on one level this all added up to a depressing and a despairing scenario, in real life the testament offered by islanders themselves remains reassuring.

6 Gesto Hospital

As noted, Gesto reached out to all parts of Skye. Besides the hospital work-load, there was considerable general practice to cover on an everyday basis, in all weather. How much more impressive, therefore, to explore the record of the very many tokens of esteem and friendship received by Dr Grant, when the time came for him to leave the island. These bear eloquent testimony to his four and a half years of good work and go to show how deeply his services were appreciated by the islanders themselves. Many of them are tributes from monoglot islanders, expressed in Gaelic, both prose and verse. Typical, too, were the personal gifts bestowed upon him at that time. For example, in 1898 there was a gift of a dining-room clock presented and hand-inscribed:

'to Dr Lachlan Grant M.D., by Mrs Carstairs as a token of gratitude for his kindness while she was ill in May and June 1898.'

Even more significant though, was the official gift from the people of Skye who presented him with a barometer and a drawing-room clock, beautifully inscribed:

'to Lachlan Grant Esq., M.D., by his friends in Skye
on leaving Gesto Hospital in August 1900.'

This splendid presentation was accompanied by hand-written verses from a local Skye poet, John Macleod, 'the Bard', a local seaman.
The tribute was composed in the Bard's native Gaelic tongue and, trans-lated, it reads:

'To Dr Grant on hearing of his great success and skill among the wretched and poor in Skye:

1   I have been told by many of the success of Dr Grant and the achieve-ments by which he is rising (in estimation) among the peasantry in the land of the bens. Every person, high and low, who was in trouble and sickness has had their gloom and grief cleverly removed by your medicines.
2   The King of Grace is showing his favour to those who are sick and hurt by sending you to Edinbane where you now reside. Your skill and talents go far above your class, giving health to every poor person who was in pain and in anguish.
3   The doctors in Edinburgh are famous for their knowledge of every disease, hurt and sore that arises in our kind – I would prefer the skill

of Dr Grant, among the sick – always expected out – to drive away their troubles.

4 I have been told you are a real gentleman and that you have much cause for being that. You are kind to every poor one who comes to you with sad and putrid sores. You are an honour to your country and I am sorry I have not your acquaintance. Many a one you are keeping alive for time to seek mortally.

John Macleod,
Gaelic Bard

7 Village Vaccination

8 'Young in Harness': Dr Grant and his pony

On being appointed assistant GP to Dr MacCalman in Oban in 1896, it was Dr Grant's first post in general practice. At this early stage of his career it appears he was backed financially by his parents, and Peter Grant had assisted in the purchase of Craigard, in Oban, as a home and base there. On Dr Grant's early onward move to Skye, to take up his Gesto appointment, further parental aid came in the form of the purchase of a pony and trap to provide the necessary mode of transport. This splendid photograph from around 1896 is set in front of Gesto Hospital and the adjoining doctor's house at Edinbane. It portrays the glossy grey pony harnessed up, and a lean young Dr Grant posed, cloaked and gloved, atop the carriage, all ready to drive out to a home visit.

4

Return to the Highlands

When Dr Bertie Simpson, who from 1889 to 1892 was Medical Officer to Ballachulish Quarries, first struck up conversation with the young 18-year-old local lad, Lachlan Grant, he could not have realised the significance of their exchange. Enquiring of the boy what he would like to do in life, Dr Simpson was told that we would like to be a doctor but only 'if my father will allow me to remain in the Highlands and practise among the people.' The encounter made a distinct impression on Dr Simpson and he did not forget these words. He was to recall them on an occasion some fifty-six years later!

At that particular stage Grant had not even entered medical school; indeed he was still to enter the Arts Faculty at Glasgow University, before his enrolment into Edinburgh University Medical School in 1889. It would seem the lad was nursing this ambition all along. If so, one has to say he was pretty single-minded about it, for he cleared with a clean pair of heels all the hurdles in his path, his medical school career studded with awards and his graduation achieved with honours. To be selected by Edinburgh's clinical chiefs to perform house physician duties at their units and clinics, and assist them personally, was grooming in action. Grant was being prepared for an academic career. It is remarkable to most people that he eschewed that option, but he did. Those, like Dr Simpson, who had better measure of the man, may not have been in the least surprised. Dr Grant, in any event, knew his own mind and was one to pursue his own ideas.

Perhaps it was in order to shake off Edinburgh's academic dust that he ventured to the USA and Canada for postgraduate study in the American and Canadian systems of healthcare and treatments. Perhaps it was to gain experience on how to cope with clinical situations in a far and distant land of frontiers, forests and harsh conditions. Whatever the explanation, the experience did buffer his transition from Edinburgh's 'ivory tower' to face the realities of remote and rural general medical practice in the Highlands.

True to himself, Dr Grant took up his first such appointment in Oban. He became GP assistant to Dr MacCalman, who had a general medical practice based in the town extending well into the surrounding countryside. He had

9 Baile à Chaolais – Village of the Narrows

known Dr MacCalman in earlier times, for the latter had been medical officer at Ballachulish for eleven years, from 1878 to 1889. Dr MacCalman would certainly have been family doctor to the Grant family at Loanfern, from the time of their arrival in the glen in 1880. Having secured a post as GP in Argyllshire, Dr Grant could rightly claim he had made 'his return home.'

Argyllshire, however, did not hold him for long. In the very year of his arrival in Oban, the Trustees of Gesto Hospital in Edinbane in Skye were advertising for a new medical officer to replace Dr Keith N. MacDonald, who was leaving. The hospital had been built in 1878 with 12 beds and it was Skye's first hospital. As already noted, on his death in 1869 Kenneth Macleod of Gesto, and latterly of Greshornish, had left a legacy of £10k from his Indian estates, to found a hospital on his native island 'for the benefit of his countrymen, the people of Skye.' Dr MacDonald was Kenneth Macleod's nephew. As the hospital enjoyed generous endowment, its trustees were in position to offer a higher than average salary to a doctor appointed to replace Dr MacDonald. It was recognised that doctor appointments to voluntary hospitals like Gesto were well rewarded, and at the time of the 1896 vacancy remuneration was sufficiently attractive for Dr Grant to submit his application. From a field of sixty-five candidates, his qualifications and qualities, as an applicant, were good enough in the eyes of the trustees for his appointment to the post to be unanimous. In taking up his appointment at Gesto Hospital Dr Grant undoubtedly made a 'return to the Highlands;' to an island, in fact. The era was historically a harsh period everywhere in the country, but especially Skye where there was widespread destitution. The crops were failing, crofting was failing, and health was suffering. Inasmuch as it existed, human shelter and sanitation was woeful. Mortality in all age groups was high; it was a fact of life that many people died without medical assistance and without certification by any qualified person.

There was rising resentment over land issues, rents, and rewards for 'improvements' tackled or labour provided. In north-west Skye these issues boiled over: there were riots, there were battles (and battle-ships in the bay), and 'martyrs' were created. Not far from Dr Grant's hospital base in Edinbane was the parish of Glendale, the crucible of troubles and the furnace for reform. John MacPherson was a legendary native figure who was central to this agitation and the legal demands it made. Without question, Lachlan Grant became acquainted with such action and activity, immersed himself in it, and honed his politics and political skills on the whetstone of cottars and crofters. His 4½-year professional engagement at Gesto Hospital and among the people of Skye must have been formative to his own developing political philosophy, views and outlook. It was bound to form the foundation to his immense involvement, years later, in related issues and organisations such as the Crofters' and Cottars'

10 Dressing the Slate at Ballachulish Quarries

Association, the Highland Development League, the Sea League, the New Deal for the Highlands, and the Caledonian Power Scheme. If one also takes account of the torrid time he himself suffered at the hands of the quarry masters and the 'lockout' dispute, one can see the factors which fashioned him to be the person he was and to fight the corners he fought. Dr Grant's remarkable baptism in the Isle of Skye drew to an end in 1900. That year marked a deterioration in his father's health and his father's impending death compelled him to return home to Ballachulish to support his mother.

The dislocation, though, meant no move away from his beloved Highlands as, by good fortune, a vacancy for a replacement medical officer to the Ballachulish Medical Quarry Company had freshly arisen. Dr Farquharson, who had filled the post after Dr Simpson left and served for six years, had decided to quit the post. It was said he had done so exactly one month before he was due to be dismissed, in any event, by the quarry company. An unpropitious back-drop?

Neither timing nor luck, however, could have dealt Dr Grant a better hand. Here he was, out of a job, looking for another close to home with seemingly slim chance of any local vacancy. So, with a local vacancy now advertised by the quarry company, the prospect of appointment was a godsend, depending on being selected, of course. The annual salary on offer for the post was set at £270 per annum, which sum in monetary terms nowadays equates to £27,400. With added income streams, the reward would be enhanced and the post deemed sufficiently attractive to be applied for. Dr Grant had good credentials: his medical qualifications were first-class, he was a native of the place, spoke their language, matched their culture and had returned home. As a matter of record, he had temporarily worked as a clerk in the quarry master's office in the years between leaving school and entering college. He seemed the ideal candidate for the post. It was the responsibility of Ballachulish Quarrymen's Medical Committee to make the appointment,★ and confirm it. Again, all members of the interview panel were familiar with him, as were the villagers. From more than sixty candidates Dr Lachlan Grant was selected as doctor to

★ Whenever a medical officer vacancy arose at the quarries it was usual practice for the quarry company to place an advertisement in the *British Medical Journal* for applicants. The following advert is the one published in the *BMJ* on 14 May 1892, when the company was in search of a doctor:

Medical Vacancies:

Ballachulish Slate works, Ballachulish – Medical Officer; unmarried. Salary £216 p.a., and general practice.

Application and testimonials till May 18th to:

Dr Campbell, Ballachulish, N.B. 1892

succeed to the vacancy and he was unanimously appointed to the office. He took up his duties on 1 August 1900 and not only did his future seem secure, he seemed well and truly set to fulfil his destiny: 'to be a doctor and return to the Highlands to practise among the people'.

11 Dr Lachlan Grant and his sisters Polly and Anna

5

Unexpected Conflict

Just as the local landscape around Ballachulish and the quarries seemed tranquil, if not serene, and everyone seemed satisfied with the medical services in place since the appointment of Dr Grant in August 1900, there came out of the clear blue sky in early June 1902, the 'bolt' that Ballachulish Slate Quarry Company had dismissed its medical officer, giving 30 days notice. Initially the issue was locally contained, but swords were drawn. When 30 days had passed and notice of termination was served on Dr Grant on 3 July 1902, blades were sharpened as conflict loomed. Still, at that stage the issue remained a 'local conflagration,' but it showed all signs of spreading as the two opposing sides defined their terms and dug in their heels. There seemed little prospect of an early end to the matter, and every expectation that it would flare up. It did. Suddenly, action burst out on all fronts and at many levels. To keep pace with events was in itself demanding, if not impossible, as the conflict generated momentum and the crisis swirled around in public, in the press, in law and in politics.

By August 1902 accounts were appearing in the local and national press reporting the 'extraordinary action' of the Ballachulish Slate Quarry Company and its attempt to get rid of their medical officer. This was taking place despite the fact that the quarrymen, from whose wages the doctor's salary was deducted, unanimously wished him to remain in post. The company directors' action against Dr Lachlan Grant caused indignation among the men, who steadfastly resolved to have no other doctor to provide care for them save him. They held the right to appoint their own doctor and refused to allow any deduction from their wages to go to any other medical officer whomsoever. On the other side, the directors insisted it was their right to choose a medical officer for their employees even if the men themselves did not wish it and that it was their right to deduct from their wages the salary payable to any doctor whom the company were to appoint. Above all the directors insisted on their right to dismiss Dr Grant from the position which he had held with the company since August 1900. The men stuck to their principles and the directors sought an interdict to prevent Dr Grant from practising in the Ballachulish area.

The salary payable to Dr Grant at the time was £270 per year, every penny of it being deducted from each and every worker's pay-packet. The directors insisted there was no injustice in their action and they were adamant it was not improper for them to dismiss their employee, the doctor, and ban him from holding any other medical appointment in the local area. Dr Grant, on the other hand, steadfastly maintained he had faithfully discharged all duties and that no grounds existed for the actions being taken against him. He further held that, as the quarrymen had unanimously passed a resolution in full support of him being retained as their medical officer, the company were acting beyond and above their legal powers in the matter. The legal teams representing the respective parties duly presented their case before the Court of Session. In December 1902 Lord Kyllachy gave his judgement. He found against Dr Grant and the quarrymen. There was widespread dissatisfaction and disbelief. The result aroused many local people and fellow countrymen and the case raged on in the national news. Journalists, editors, politicians, doctors, clergymen and ordinary individuals piled in with their support for Dr Grant. It made most uncomfortable reading for those who were out to demolish him. A point made by many, and made repeatedly, was that if this indeed was the law, then the law itself needed changing. In a short interval of time, unsurprisingly, a legal appeal was lodged. Once more the case was pored over and the legal niceties teased out at length by the finest of legal minds.

Incredible though it seemed to a great many people, the decision of the Court of Appeal was to firmly uphold the original judgement. This result simply served to reinforce the sense of injustice felt by the losing party and his many supporters. They were all of one mind: it was necessary to seek justice from the highest court in the land, the House of Lords.

As previously stated, there was a flurry of action and activity going on at various times and in various places. It is essential to the narrative to track these events and keep an eye on them so as to cover the canvass completely.

Locally, with regard to operations at Ballachulish slate quarries, one notes that Dr Grant's appointment in August 1900 was properly and constitutionally carried out. Dr Farquharson had tendered his resignation, albeit thirty days before the quarry company was about to dismiss him from the post, and the company had openly advertised for his successor. The medical committee, an elected body comprising the quarry-master and seven quarries, had entire control over all matters pertaining to the medical officer for the quarries, including his appointment and salary, which traditionally had been met by deductions from the wages of the quarrymen. The medical committee performed its duty in the matter and Dr Grant had been the unanimously chosen applicant. All parties involved, including Dr Grant, were satisfied with such arrangements, and all parties moved forward in that frame of mind from August 1900 until the unilateral and unexpected developments of June 1902.

While anger and resentment was welling up among the men and their equally stressed families, the quarry company pressed ahead with its chosen course of action and on 3 July 1902 went on to issue a notice of termination of contract to Dr Grant.

The local atmosphere was filled with accusation, claim and counter-claim, and workers' meetings and public meetings were advertised. In all the turmoil Dr Grant, who was at its vortex, was not short of support. Immediately to his defence sprang two leading worthies: local leaders and heavyweights, Dr W Dunlop Anderson of Ardsheal, a retired doctor and local landowner, and the Rev. Duncan MacMurchy, minister of the United Free Church. A torrent of post office telegrams of support was received daily at Barr's Stores and Post Office in Loanfern. One telegram from Dr DPM Farquharson, the previous medical officer at the quarries from 1894 to 1900, roundly declared:

"Have learned today with surprise and regret of brother's [Dr Grant] dismissal. Hope, however, the quarrymen and outsiders will not allow such gross interference with their rights, not alone for Dr Grant's sake but on principle, if men and outsiders tell him to accept resignation from none but them, or let them re-appoint him, he should fight. I would with greatest pleasure. Wishing cause success."

From (Dr) Farquharson

08.07.1902

Word began to circulate as to what the reasons for dismissal were: that adverse reporting on the company's housing state was 'increasing in volume and tone, apace;' that Dr Grant was not devoting all his time to his quarry medical officer duties; that Dr Grant's brother had posted up notices claiming the quarry company was infringing the Truck Acts. The second reason, as listed, was certainly given by the company's chairman when he attempted to explain the actions taken by the company's directors. The third reason was unfounded, as in fact it was Mr Angus Clark, secretary to the quarrymen's medical committee, and future leader of the local quarries' trade union, who had done the billing.

Interesting speculation also arose to the effect that the true reason for the extent and depth of the disagreement between Grant and MacColl, the quarry manager, was a local rivalry as to which of them should dominate the local community in status. It seems, however, the public at large did not believe there could be much substance to that explanation.

Sensibly, the quarrymen protected themselves in their actions. One early act was for the men to assemble to call a meeting to elect a 'new and reconstituted' medical committee of nine men. These were Mr Alex MacLaren, Mr Peter MacKenzie, Mr Ronald MacColl, Mr Donald MacColl, Mr Donald Downie, Mr Alex Stewart, Mr Alex MacTaggart and Mr Angus Clark, with Mr Donald MacMillan elected as chairman. Having convened in this manner, they resolved to appoint their own medical officer.

A mass meeting on 8 July 1902, held in the square at Ballachulish, sent a clear and determined message to all shareholders in the Ballachulish Slate Quarry Company. It read:

"That this meeting representative of all inhabitants of Ballachulish and District regret that Dr Grant, medical officer of the slate quarries, has been dismissed at a month's notice from the post which he has held, and from the duties which he has so ably and faithfully discharged for the past two years."

Prior to the mass meeting Dr Grant himself had drawn up a neatly presented document, hand-written in ink, reading as follows:

1 'That this meeting representative of Ballachulish and district has heard with the deepest regret that Dr Grant, medical officer of the slate quarries, has been dismissed at a month's notice from the post which he has held, and from the duties which he has so ably and faithfully discharged for the past two years.
2 That the company be respectfully requested to reconsider their decision in respect to Dr Grant.
3 That though they recognise the legality of the present system of appointment of a medical officer, it is a matter of regret to the meeting that the employees of the quarries should not have some voice in his selection, in which case his dismissal would be the result of the vote of the majority, and could give rise to no such grave and widespread dissatisfaction as that now evinced.
4 That these resolutions be forwarded to the directors of the company.'

The meeting and its outcome were widely reported in the press both locally and nationally. The medical press were just as interested, particularly regarding some areas of the dispute such as the employment aspect and the hiring and firing of any medical practitioner.

The chairman and the company directors were keeping a close watch over matters as they operated a lockout of the quarries and sealed the quarry gates, thus preventing any worker entry (not that it was their desire to do so) while the dispute smouldered. Officially, on 3 July 1902 that lockout came to pass. All along the way it was not predictable how long the dispute would last and it appeared to one and all that only the law would solve the matter.

[The shareholders in the Ballachulish Quarry Company Ltd., at the time, and with whom Dr Grant and the quarrymen had issue, are listed (along with their respective shareholdings) opposite.]

In an attempt to address, if not to arrest, the tide of local anger against the slate company and the tarnished reputation being painted to the nation, it was inevitable that there would be a response from the chairman of the Ballachulish Slate Quarry Company Ltd. An explanation was offered in the local press, *The Oban Times*. Leaflets were also widely distributed among the residents of Ballachulish and district outlining the company's position.

The directors of the company and its chairman (Col. E D Malcolm C.B.) evidently could not have anticipated the adverse public reaction the decision to dismiss the doctor from his post would bring, and the sheer weight and welter of criticism brought upon their heads. In a way there seemed to be a sense of surprise, even hurt, displayed by the chairman but the reaction was interpreted and read by his opponents as simply 'pure arrogance.' The charge by the quarrymen and their families, that the doctor has been dismissed 'without any reason given', had stung or stirred the Colonel into action and, on 26 July 1902, the following letter was despatched to the press. Col. Malcolm was unrepentant and plainly in no mood to take prisoners.

'When Dr Grant was appointed the directors of the quarry company came voluntarily under an obligation to secure him a certain fixed sum on money as salary annually. The medical gentleman at Ballachulish has always been a quarry doctor in the first instance, but the country is getting filled up, more people are living around, and of late the quarry doctor, it appears to the quarry directors of the company, has been inclined to take on work which makes it necessary that he should be more and more absent from the neighbourhood of the quarries, and the directors do not like it. When the present gentleman came to Ballachulish he signed an agreement with the directors, which agreement either party might end by giving one month's notice. Most people stick to a bargain, but Dr Grant, or more likely injudicious friends, have raised a cry of dismissal, cruel ill-treatment, and so forth, and have not put before you the facts of the case fully. Have you been told that Dr Grant has put it out of his power to practise in the district on the termi-

Register of Shareholders in Ballachulish Quarries (at September 1901) and shareholdings:

No. held	Shareholder	Occupation	Resident of
30	Bruce, Edward	Contractor	Edinburgh
10	Bruce, Edward Jr.	Contractor	Edinburgh
13	Buik, John Hendry	Rope Manufacturer	Wick
60	Belfrage, Andrew W.	Civil Engineer	Edinburgh
12	Buik, Mrs Elizabeth Caldwell	Wife of JHB	Wick
1	Brown, Archibald	Manager, Lloyds Bank	Cardiff Docks
1	Brown, Duncan Campbell	Bank Agent, BOS	Oban
5	Boyle, Mrs Ann Easter Millidge		Edinburgh
5	Cook, James Adam	Insurance Manager	Liverpool
30	Campbell, Hugh		Edinburgh
10	Dewar, Thomas		Leith
20	Low, John	Slater	Edinburgh
2	Low, Edward Bruce	SSC	Edinburgh
12	Low, Alex Bruce	Doctor of Medicine	Sunderland
63	Lindsay, James Cooper		Edinburgh
60	Malcolm, Edward D.	Colonel, C.B.	Poltalloch
60	Mungall, Henry	Coal Merchant	Edinburgh
20	Mailer, William		Glasgow
20	Millidge, Edwin	Rtd. Jeweller	Edinburgh
11	MacColl, Archibald	Quarrymaster	Ballachulish
20	Newton, Wm. Watson	Slate Merchant	Glasgow
6	Nisbet, Miss Christina		Edinburgh
20	Ogilvy, Alex	Slater	Leith
10	Paterson, John	Merchant	Edinburgh
13	Shaw, Thomas	Advocate	Edinburgh
1	Stewart, William.	Bank Agent	Lochgilphead
50	Thomson, Robt. James		Edinburgh
30	Wilson, James	Builder	Edinburgh

In regard to the company and its dividends, it was reported that in 1902 the company was constituted with a nominal capital of £30,000 in £50 shares. However, the actual amount invested was recorded at only £17 per share, the capital paid up on each share issued. In September 1901 the sum of only £10,200 of the £30,000 capital had been paid up. The total company dividend paid per share at the end of the year 1900 and, based on £50 invested per share, was 'entered' as £3.14s.6d. per share.

nation of his engagement, and that he has barred himself by law from accepting any appointment from you? If you want to know why the directors are not satisfied with the recent agreement, I will inform you that it was not sufficiently binding to prevent Dr Grant from taking work on at a distant granite quarry, he taking the place of another medical gentleman who has looked after the men there for many years. Moreover, a clause which was drawn up so that the doctor's address might be known if he was going away got less and less attended to, and the directors felt that in your interest the agreement should be kept.

I would remind you that Dr Grant was recently appointed by the directors, who took a good deal of trouble to see that as far as certificates go he was a competent man, and it is not to be supposed that the directors will be less careful another time. In conclusion, I must express my great regret that people unconnected with the quarries have interfered, to make that which might have been arranged impossible of arrangement.

Yours truly,
E.D. Malcolm,
Chairman'

A lengthy reply and response was generated and it appeared in the *Oban Telegraph and Express* on 15 August 1902:

'A phase of this case was developed last week, when a printed manifesto, signed by Col. Malcolm, was posted throughout Ballachulish. What makes this document important is the fact that it professes to give the reasons why the company have dismissed Dr Grant. I shall give the reasons, with a few necessary explanations, and leave your readers to judge whether they are sufficient to justify the action of the directors.

The complaints are two in number. The first contained in these words, which I quote from the manifesto: 'if you want to know why the directors are not satisfied with the recent agreement, I will inform you that it was not sufficiently binding to prevent Dr Grant from taking work on at a distant granite quarry.' I would ask, why should Dr Grant be punished because they were not satisfied with their own agreement, under which Dr Grant was at liberty to take up any practice in the district? Further, I would ask, are we to understand from the above statement that if the company have the power, they will prevent the quarry doctor from attending any patients at the granite quarries, which are only four miles away, although Col. Malcolm claims to call this distant? The next nearest doctor is fourteen miles away. In the event of a case of sudden and serious illness or accident occurring at Lettermore, the slate quarries' doctor would be prohibited from attending, with the possible result that death might ensure before medical aid could be summoned from Port Appin or Fort William. Let the people of Lettermore take note of this. It is a most serious question for them.

The second complaint is to the following effect: 'a clause which was drawn up so that the doctor's address might be known if he was going away got less and less attended to, and the directors felt that in your interest the agreement should be kept.' Now, after such an explicit statement, your readers will no doubt be very much surprised to learn that there is not one word in the agreement about the doctor leaving his address, when going away. This is only one of several inaccurate statements, most damaging to Dr Grant, which have been made in the course of the dispute. I am etc.

LAROCH'

While the debate ran on in public and in the press, and as the case itself trundled on through the courts of the land, local meetings were convened to address the important issue of fund-raising. The quarrymen well realised that justice does not come cheaply, and industrial action comes at a cost. They knew they faced steep legal costs and families would meet with much individual hardship. A vital step was to raise money by appeal to a very wide, and hopefully receptive, public and in their first move the men formed a Medical Committee Appeal Fund ('the Appeal Fund') and a Quarrymen's Defence Fund ('the Relief Fund'). One fund was to meet all legal fees and related expenses to do with the legal action, and the other to relieve hardship among the quarrymen who were out of work, and their dependent families. In both cases it was considered necessary to set up the appeal as a national one, and indeed the hope was for an international response. From the outset it was made plain that it was not to be a 'cap-in-hand' exercise. Volunteers were prepared to put in a mountain of work towards organising large fund-raising ceilidhs, gatherings, rallies and public meetings, not only in the towns and cities of Scotland but also those of England where Scots, especially, flocked to support the cause. The effort was countrywide, from Lochaber to London. The Scottish and Highland Societies abroad, in countries to which Highlanders had emigrated, or to which their ancestors had been 'cleared,' were included in the appeal. Countries like the United States of America, Canada, Australia and New Zealand were especially responsive and generous. One could safely say that wherever in the Commonwealth there was a Scot, monetary contribution was forthcoming. That said, the main stream of funds flowed in from the homeland.

Unsurprisingly, there were many early demands on the Relief Fund as cases of eviction being threatened against quarriers' families came to light. The families of such as Donald MacColl, John MacColl, Alex MacLaren and Alex MacTaggart, were primarily involved and, as they were all well-known committee members and ardent supporters of Dr Grant, vindictiveness by the company had entered the big picture.

It is most interesting to read through the various individual contributions that were sent in to the appeal. All donations were acknowledged in the press and thus made public. In certain circumstances the donations were made and the sum kept anonymous, but recorded in the treasurer's ledger; for example, Mrs Charles Stirling of Carnoch House of Glencoe, is down as 'contributed.' There were donations collected and submitted by the good folk of Tighnabruaich in the Cowal area, where Dr Grant and his family often spent holiday times and where the family of William and Mary Paton owned an imposing holiday home, Wellpark, and the other substantial properties of Mountainside and Sherbrooke. In more open and specific fashion, though, were donations such as the following:

Dr J B Simpson (a former local GP)	donated	£ 1. 1s.
Dr T S Clouston (Edinburgh consultant)	donated	1. 1s.
Dr DPM Farquharson (former quarry MO)	donated	5. 5s.
Prof. Argyll Robertson (Edinburgh)	donated	1. 1s.
Mrs Chinnery Haldane	donated	10. 10s.
Broderick Chinnery Haldane	donated	3. 3s.

These entries are but a tiny sample of contributors and, as accounts reveal, the total sum raised was spectacular: true to the Scots saying, 'mony a mickle maks a muckle.'

The appeal committees had as their chairman Mr Duncan MacMillan, Mr Angus Clark as their secretary, and Mr Peter MacKenzie as the all-important treasurer. When, at the end of the day, the case had been won and the auditors had signed off the accounts, the quarrymen, their supporters, and the many friends who contributed could be justifiably proud of themselves. It was a massive undertaking in the first place, but the exercise had turned into a remarkable achievement.

The accounts when audited and presented, read as follows:

Statement of the whole Income & Expenditure of the Ballachulish Quarrymen's Appeal Fund from January 1903 to December 1903

	£	s.	d.
To subscriptions received and duly acknowledged in the press	895	01	11
Expenditure:			
For Medical Club's Law Action	271	00	05
For Dr Grant's Law Action	388	08	07
Committee's Travelling Expenses, Printing, Telegrams,			
Postage, Stationery etc.,	66	15	01
Total	726	04	01
To Cash in National Bank of Scotland	135	09	05
To Cash in Treasurer's hands	33	01	11
Total	895	01	11

We have carefully examined the Treasurer's books with relative vouchers and found them to be correct.

Sig: Archibald MacCallum
Donald Clark

Ballachulish, 15th November 1904

When one views the heavy legal engagement in this conflict, by both sides, it is no surprise that so much fund-raising had to be undertaken. Serious sums of money were at stake. Fund-raising aside, the quarrymen and all Dr Grant's supporters from near and far held numerous public meetings to drum up support, to fan publicity for their cause and to demonstrate to the world their unity of purpose, determination to win and the iniquity they suffered at the hands of a harsh regime, the Ballachulish Quarry Company Ltd. It was an example of impressive and effective campaigning for justice. At a meeting early on in the campaign Dr Farquharson, who had formerly practised in the community and who was now in practice in Manchester and holidaying in the district at this time, exhorted the gathering thus:

'This is not a question of Dr Grant nor any other man. It is a question of your rights as men and citizens. When I was amongst you, as you know, I always urged upon you to combine and be true to each other. I say the same to you now. This action by the company has simply brought you your opportunity. The appointment of the doctor is only one of your rights. There are many others. Stand together, be true to yourselves and to the committee of true men whom you have appointed, and nothing can prevent you winning. Stand together!'

At these meetings, successive speakers from platform and from hall floor contributed heartfelt testimonies to Dr Grant. He was 'a great favourite wherever he practised.' He was 'president of the Ballachulish Camanachd Club.' He was 'the best student of his year.' He had 'the most impressive record; he was assistant to Prof. Argyll Robertson; he was MO at Gesto Hospital; and had excelled in these posts.' The praise was deafening and at many of these rallies the war cry of the Clan Grant was raised to the rafters: 'Stand Fast, Craigellachie!' A rousing display of this kind did wonders for morale and, in a sense, served to intimidate those in the opposing camp.

The Ballachulish Quarry Company took its case to the Court of Session in Edinburgh on 6 November 1902. On 18 December Lord Kyllachy, presiding, gave his judgement, which was an adverse one to Dr Grant and the quarrymen. The losing party in the dispute, however, did not waste any time and in good PR fashion issued a terse statement as follows:

'Dr Grant of Ballachulish and his friends are not in any way disconcerted by the adverse decision in the Court of Session. An appeal has already been launched.'

Sure and certain, the appeal was prepared and in early January 1903 Dr Grant and the quarrymen were granted leave to appeal. The appeal to the Inner House of the Court of Session was heard before a bench of four senior judges.

Again, the opposing parties had to bide their time. The Court of Appeal took five months to deliberate and consider the case before it, not delivering its judgement until 29 May 1903. Again the finding was in favour of the company, upholding the original judgement. While the news did come as a blow, it also served to stiffen the resolve of the quarrymen, Dr Grant, and his ardent supporters. They were absolutely clear in their mind, and firmly decided, that they had to head for the highest court in the land, the House of Lords. They were stoutly encouraged by their friends and supporters to do so and messages in this vein poured in from all directions, from countless countries, and from lots of organisations, by letter, line and post office telegraph. Again, the Grant war cry was to be repeated on the bulk of them. Appeal to the House of Lords was lodged without delay, on 27 June 1903 to be precise. A deposit of £200, as required by law, was lodged along with it.

How Dr Grant and the quarrymen around him coped with the immense pressure a legal action of this magnitude was bound to exert on them is well beyond admiration. The experience undoubtedly stressed them both individually and collectively. There was the attendant, and mounting, cost of legal fees and expenses, and of income loss besides. The safety net for them all must have been the mass, unwavering support from the public, locally and from afar. At any rate, both parties went right to the wire. In December 1903, attitudes on both sides of the divide somehow, unexpectedly, thawed and the decision to withdraw the appeal just as their Lordships were on the point of examining the case, facilitated progress sufficiently for them to steel themselves to instead resolve the dispute by negotiation. At that moment the 'famous,' or infamous, 'Ballachulish Lockout' effectively dissolved and everyone affected was set to get their life back to some semblance of normality once more. With respect to Dr Lachlan Grant, however, the date of resolution could not be officially recognised until it was confirmed in a press announcement in the *British Medical Journal* on 20 January 1904, when the following entry was there for the whole world to read and absorb:

'APPOINTMENT

Grant, Lachlan M.D. C.M. Edin. Reappointed Medical Officer to the Ballachulish Quarriers' Medical Club, vice A. Dingwall Kennedy M.B. Ch.B. Glasg. Resigned.'

In splendid style, it seems, Dr Grant set off on holiday and arranged for Dr Kennedy to step into the breach during his absence on leave. Once he returned, Dr Lachlan Grant was back in harness, without prejudice to himself or the quarrymen. It was back too to the days they had known and enjoyed before 3 June 1902. Dr Grant certainly made it clear that there was work to do. For the next forty years or so, he was to go on doing it.

The news of Dr Grant's reinstatement, without penalty of any kind, was greeted in all quarters with relief and jubilation in equal measure. His medical colleagues, past and present, inundated him with generous messages of congratulations and best wishes for the future. These included his university tutors, lecturers and distinguished professors. As noted, many of them had earlier nobly contributed to the Appeal Fund. In everyone's eyes the exercise had been an investment well worth backing.

From January 1904 conflict was no longer a word on people's lips. The year did have its ups and downs in regard to the world markets and the slate trade, but business continued and men were in full-time work. By the end of 1904, however, the markets had taken a nosedive and there was great concern regarding the viability of the quarries. In June 1905 it was real enough to raise fears of closure of the quarries 'for a time.' This led to proposals to reduce the working week to 4 days, lower wages and restrict employment to one man per household. The employment situation got very messy and divisive. The quarrymen laid the blame squarely at the quarry manager's door and so Mr Archibald MacColl became the target of the men's anger. Emotions ran high and erupted in a serious act of mobbing and rioting at MacColl's home at Laroch House on 15 July 1905. The men and their families had had enough. They pursued 'regime change': a change of manager at the quarries and expulsion of MacColl from the district. 'Work should not be accepted from the present manager,' they insisted. As a result of the fracas outside the manager's home, twelve quarrymen faced charges at Oban Sheriff Court on 12 August 1905; five were found guilty and fined £5 each, two found guilty and fined £3, and five were found not guilty. It was some consolation, though, to hear what their actions had achieved. Firstly, MacColl did resign his post. Secondly, Col. Malcolm resigned as chairman. Thirdly, the respected Mr Hugh MacColl was placed in charge of the company's affairs locally. The result was cathartic. Agreement between the employer and the employees was signed in mid-August of 1905 and work resumed on a 5–day–week basis. But in regard to slate quarrying generally, and Ballachulish Slate Quarries in particular, the road ahead remained a rocky one and any euphoria was short-lived. At an Extraordinary General Meeting of the company in August 1907 it was decided to call in the liquidators. This action left the local slate quarry industry in deep crisis, and everyone entertained grave doubts if salvation would ever come their way.

To recap slightly regarding the prolonged industrial dispute from 1902–1904 and the subsequent one of 1905, it is to be noted that the second dispute lasted only five months from its onset to its date of settlement, whereas the more notable first dispute lasted eighteen whole months in total. It is also important to appreciate that Dr Grant, who was the central figure in the first dispute, had no role to play in the second conflict, and that dispute had no direct personal bearing on him. Nonetheless, he gave all the support he could to the quarrymen, who were involved in the 1905 industrial action, and likely helped to mentor them over the period. He was not the person to forget the fierce loyalty the quarrymen offered him or to turn his back on them. In both disputes all parties must have been glad to have the muscle of Angus Clark at their back. He became the trade union leader of the quarrymen at the time of the lockout and after Keir Hardie's visit; but Clark was more than a trade unionist, he was a man of far greater vision.

THE BALLACHULISH QUARRIES' MEDICAL COMMITTEE

The Quarriers' Medical Committee, otherwise 'the medical committee,' was an important, influential and useful body, which had control over all aspects of the appointment of the medical officer, including the terms and conditions of service relating to his appointment as well as the remuneration and payments to be made as regards to medical work performed on behalf of the company, the quarrymen and families in Ballachulish and the district. The committee operated under a constitution with a membership of eight elected representatives and the quarry manager, who in effect was the 'company's man' on the committee. The eight members were elected by the quarrymen and were there to represent the interests of the workforce and families. The committee had a chairman elected from the eight representing the quarrymen. The curious feature is the representation of company interest on the committee, since the doctor's wages and expenses were met in full from deductions from the quarrymen's weekly wage packet; not a single penny came from company coffers. A case of representation without taxation, surely. It is no surprise that the workmen were so indignant that their medical officer had been dismissed, unilaterally, by the company in 1903. Dr Grant was, after all, their medical officer.

THE BALLACHULISH QUARRIES' MEDICAL OFFICERS:
1878–1945

If one surveys the calibre of doctor appointed, successively, to the post from 1878 up to the time Dr Grant was appointed in 1900, one can be satisfied that 'the committee' discharged its duties responsibly.

From 1878 to 1889, for example, the incumbent was Dr MacCalman who, when he left in 1889, set up as general practitioner in Oban. He was the local GP at Ballachulish at the time the Grant family came to settle in the area and would have been family doctor to the Grants, and to Lachlan Grant himself for some nine years. As noted earlier, Dr Grant was to be Dr MacCalman's GP assistant in Oban in 1896, albeit briefly.

After Dr MacCalman's departure to Oban, the committee appointed Dr James Simpson from Golspie. He served as the quarries' medical officer over the period 1889 to 1892, close to being a four-year stint. He was highly regarded by his patients as a reliable and trusted professional man. Dr James Bertie Simpson was one of a medical dynasty of Highland doctors from East Sutherland, who loyally served the population around Golspie. He contributed much to the social fabric of the local district while at Ballachulish, including being very supportive to the parish church of St Munda, whose records even show that, in reply to an invitation extended to him to attend their social evening, 'an acceptance had been received from Dr James B Simpson, the local Medical Practitioner, written in his beautiful round hand.' That trait must be in the genes for his grandson, Dr Michael Simpson, writes comparably: quite atypical of most of the medical profession. Dr Bertie Simpson was observant, with an eye for detail, and kept notes meticulously. He was also of a literary mind. His friendship with Dr Lachlan Grant is on record and (years later) his obituary of Dr Grant, in the *BMJ*, is a model contribution. Dr Simpson's act was a hard one to follow, but it was, and by a totally different type of character: a force of nature.

Dr D.P.M. Farquharson served as M.O. for six years from 1894 to 1900, going about his duties in a confident outspoken way, saying whatever had to be said. His unease over the prevailing local housing conditions and public health matters, and the role of the quarry company in all of that he made widely known and openly voiced. He endorsed all criticisms made by the Argyllshire MOH, Dr Roger McNeill, in this area. He regularly took to the public platform and in the strife years of 1903 and 1904, he surfaced in support of his successor, Dr Grant, to turn up the heat on the opposition. He gave generously to the quarrymen's appeal fund. It was said of him that he resigned his post in 1900 one month before the quarry company were to sack him!

Whatever else, he was unquestionably the patient's friend, and a staunch medical advocate to have on one's side. In August 1900, the baton passed to Dr Lachlan Grant, and his long and distinguished record is laid out before us. However, his passing in 1945 meant he did not live to witness the closure of the Ballachulish Quarries, which had played so large a part in his life, and tugged his emotions.

12 Ballachulish Quarrymen's Medical Committee
and Medical Officer (Dr Grant), October 1902

Alex Stewart   Don MacColl   Alex McTaggart
        Peter MacKenzie   Alex McLaren   Donald Downie
            (Treas)

    Don MacMillan   Dr Lachlan Grant   Angus Clark
     (Chairman)   (Secretary)

6

Passions, Politics and Social Reforms

Lachlan Grant was passionate, political and innately a reformer. At what age he developed his ideas is not clear, but examination of his journey through life and his experience en route is a helpful path to take in search for clues to revealing the overall picture. It is also of value to draw on his ancestry and antecedents and to note such qualities as may peer through that lattice.

Firstly, one realises that Lachlan Grant was not born a Highlander. His life till the age of nine years was distinctly Scottish industrial town-based. It was certainly the case that his paternal grandfather was of Highland stock, indeed, of 'true Highland' stock, from Culbin near Dingwall in Ross-shire. Grand-father Grant was a native Gaelic speaker, the only member in their Johnstone-based household over two generations who could claim to be. Thus young Lachlan would have had no exposure at all to the land of the Gael except possibly through the 'tales of a grandfather' told on the knee.

Likely, the first unforgettable experience of his early life would have come in 1878, when the City of Glasgow Bank collapse led to the bankruptcy of the family's business. Lachlan Grant was then seven years old, and sufficiently aware of the stresses so generated within the family circle. It was certain to register with him. The support of relatives would have made an impression too, as would the subsequent uprooting from their established home in a busy town setting to the wilds and wonders of Glencoe. Settling into so alien an environment would remain memorable. Moreover, he was going headlong into a very Gaelic world. Virtually the whole of North Lorn was a Gaelic-speaking area at the time and genuinely Gaidhealach, to a degree that the natural language of the playground was Gaelic and Gaelic would have been the first language of his classmates.

When Lachlan and his brother William enrolled at Ballachulish Public School on 26 April 1880, that was his new world. Once inside the classroom, ironically, the setting was quite the reverse; the children were having English drummed into them and Gaelic squeezed out of them! It must have been a trifle confusing for young minds back in the late nineteenth century. The local village experience was predictably more balanced and helpful to development towards a bilingual world. Adults in the family would also have been required to develop a working skill in the language so as to be the better integrated in the community. Immersion in the Gaelic language and culture was, therefore, on the cards for the two generations of Grants. Also, being part of so close-knit a community was no bad thing for a young family with a public role to play. One can easily envisage how a bright child like Lachlan would readily morph into a confident young Highland laddie. His education, of course, took off impressively and his medical training was undoubtedly to expand his horizons. The university and hospital circles in which he was about to dwell would certainly serve him well and mature him to be an educated, well-rounded personality. Once he graduated, of course, he was fledged: confident enough in mind to hold and express opinions of his own.

Most likely, Dr Grant's next big test was his physical translation to the medical practice in Skye. The passions and the political debates that raged on that island in the late nineteenth century, along with the very evident social reforms being cried out for, would have been etched on his mind from early days in the post. Being nigh on five years in such a political crucible would inevitably help fashion and fix his outlook and views, moulding them to what they came to be, and fire his passion to become just as intense as those of his more hoary-headed mentors in the tortured island. His professional working experience in Skye from 1896 to 1900 would have been a real eye-opener and mind-changer for him, so dreadfully dire was the social distress being witnessed.

Edinbane village lay close to the parish of Glendale, a community at the forefront of the crofters' struggle – the fight for crofters' rights, for security of tenure, for land settlement and land reform. Riots took place there and battles were fought over these issues. Local men were hauled before the country's courts of law and imprisoned for their actions in regard to these matters. Dr Grant lived close enough to the people there to have listened to their grievances and taken on board details of the issues at stake. He would have met and conversed with John MacPherson, universally known 'the Glendale Martyr,' who was the prime radical of his day. Similarly, in other parts of Skye such as Braes, the fight for rights flared defiantly. There can be no doubt, therefore, that his five-year immersion in the politics of the Skye crofters honed Dr Grant's political beliefs and stoked many of his passions. His future successive fights with officialdom in his later years were all on similar issues and along the same lines. The inescapable conclusion is that the Skye experience politicised him and turned him to embrace Liberalism; radicalised him and turned him to address the land rights reforms; burnished him and turned him to advance human rights issues and reforms in social matters like health, housing and employment. The islanders had sown the seed that was to flourish forever within him. Thus Dr Grant became a leading reformer, a prominent voice and a beacon of light for others to follow, in pursuit of solutions to enlighten people, to lighten their burden and improve the human condition.

Dr Grant was 31 years of age when the first Ballachulish quarry dispute broke out. He was at the very centre of it and, importantly, the quarrymen were as one behind him. Reading about and studying that stressful episode will readily convince one how huge an impact the experience would have had on those involved. It stress-tested many qualities: patience, persistence, endurance, mental and physical prowess, strength of character and personal beliefs. Again, it was a formative experience for Dr Grant; many of life's lessons he learned from it and took to heart. When, in later years, it came to Dr Grant's pursuit of his political passions and social reforms, all these past personal experiences were to serve him well. He was by then seasoned and confident: he led from the front.

The first campaign Grant got into after the quarries' settlement was the business of improving the life of crofters and cottars. He was keenly aware of their plight. Being a well-read man, he knew of struggles and solutions evolving in other Celtic nations, especially Ireland, so he set out with like-minded associates and held a public meeting at Connel, near Oban on 12 May 1906. This was the inaugural meeting of the Highland Crofters' and Cottars' Association. Platform speakers were the Rev. Malcolm MacCallum, Dr Lachlan Grant, and Mr Archibald McLaren as secretary. A constitution and rules were drawn up and approved, and later a pamphlet was produced and published for wider circulation. In that fashion the organisation was fledged: to campaign for much sought after improvements to crofting legislation, the acquisition and nationalisation of land and 'unionising' of crofters and cottars as a body to be the more effective in pursuit of their aims. These objectives drew very much on Dr Grant's own personal experience at the time of his legal fight with the quarries company and the vital part the formation of a local trade union (as advised by Keir Hardie MP) played in focusing people to a purpose. The Highland Crofters' and Cottars' Association aimed to set up branches in various settlements throughout the Highlands and Islands, and did so.

The next passion involved the pursuit of political solutions to the problems of the medical services that were struggling, and failing, in their efforts to cover the Highlands and Islands and its people. Much agitation had taken place across the country, pricking the conscience of Government, with the result that an official HM Treasury Committee was set up early in 1912 to examine such plight. This was an issue dear to Dr Grant's heart and an exercise in which he and his socially progressive colleagues were itching to be involved. Under the inspiring chairmanship of Sir John Dewar, the Liberal MP for Inverness-shire, an equally talented team of members were appointed to serve on the committee. On 11 July 1912 they stepped forth to carry out their important task. Their geographic remit set was to be 'the counties of Argyll, Caithness, Inverness, Ross and Cromarty, Sutherland, Orkney and Shetland, and from the Highlands of Perthshire, comprising the area in which isolation, topographical and climatic difficulties, and straitened financial circumstances are found most generally in combination, and, therefore, this was generally the area within which the question of adequate medical provision is most pressing.'

Evidence was gathered by sending questionnaires to 102 doctors and 158 other persons and collating responses; also by an itinerary of meetings, before invited witnesses, at set locations, namely, Lerwick in Shetland, Kirkwall in Orkney and Fair Isle, Thurso in Caithness, Bettyhill and Rhiconnich in Sutherlandshire; Stornoway and Garrynahine in the island Lewis; Tarbert, Harris; Lochmaddy in North Uist; and at Kyle of Lochalsh, Perth and Oban. In addition, meetings were held in Edinburgh and Glasgow and a vast collection of available published reports and papers were reviewed. It was by anyone's standard a thorough exercise.

On 28 October 1912 in Oban, Dr Grant was called as witness before the Dewar Committee on its visit there. His evidence was to be of crucial relevance and importance. He not only presented a detailed list of deficiencies in the system but also brought before the committee just as detailed a list of solutions to be applied. In this respect it appears his performance rode well above those of most other contributors. He cited the main lot of problems as being no security of tenure for doctors, inadequate housing, inadequate income, no access to appropriate transport, a poor telephone system, inability to afford locum cover and as a result, no holidays, and no professional post-graduate training to be expected. The recruitment of nurses and their organisation as one united service was required, along with new plans for community hospital building. All this, he averred, had to be brought together as one universal state service.

When, at the end of December 1912, the Dewar Committee presented its considered list of recommendations to the government, the list included every request and suggestion that Dr Lachlan Grant had submitted. What gave him and his professional colleagues even greater satisfaction was the swift response of government: the Houses of Parliament gave the nod of approval, without dissent. Thus, in early 1913 the Highlands and Islands Medical Service (HIMS) was established to deliver these objectives. Almost at a stroke, a passionately held political aim and a much-needed social reform had been achieved. The HIMS proved its worth, gaining the respect and admiration of other countries, as well as of the UK itself. It came to be recognised as the template for the National Health Service in this country, when founded in 1948. Quite poignantly, that was an event Dr Grant was not to witness: he died in early 1945. As a tribute to the Dewar Committee, and the magnificent work it performed, it seems reasonable to give an outline of its appointed members, able and diligent as they were. In brief, this Treasury Committee was served by the following, most interesting persons:

Chairman: Sir John Dewar, Liberal MP for Inverness-shire

Secretary: Mr Murdoch Beaton M.A. An Inspector under the Health Insurance Commission. Born in Ardelve, near Kyle of Lochalsh, he was a fisherman's son. Educated at the Aberdeen Grammar School, he entered Aberdeen University and graduated with an M.A. degree. In WWI, he served in the Cameron Highlanders, rising to the rank of Lt. Colonel. After the war he became a civil servant, initially based in Inverness and latterly in Edinburgh. He died in 1948, the year the NHS was launched in the UK.

13 Sir John Dewar

Secretary's Assistant: Miss Tolmie A civil servant, who acted as Mr Beaton's assistant and helped in the work of recording the oral evidence and preparing the report for publication. She was looked upon as being exceptionally efficient in her task.

Committee: The committee was one of many talents drawn from well-regarded people whose knowledge of the Highlands and Islands, and of their own localities, was immense, detailed and intimate. The members were:

Mr Andrew Lindsay: served as Convener of the County of Sutherland.
Mr Charles Orrock: lived in Stornoway, and was estate manager or chamberlain on Lewis for the estate owner, Sir James Matheson.
Dr Leslie MacKenzie: was a medically qualified man, who, appropriately, served the committee. At the time of appointment he was a Local Government Board of Scotland member.
Dr J. L. McVail: When appointed, Dr McVail was deputy chairman of Scottish Insurance Commission and he brought such expertise to the team.

14 Dewar Committee
Back row: Andrew Lindsay; Charles Orrock; Dr Leslie MacKenzie;
Murdoch Beaton; Dr J. L. McVail; J. Cullen Grierson; Dr A. C. Miller

Front row: Sir John Dewar; unknown; Miss Tolmie;
The Marchioness of Tullibardine; J. L. Robertson LL.D

Mr J. Cullen Grierson: From the far flung Northern Isles, he was Convener of the County of Shetland.

Dr Alexander C. Miller M.B. C.M. M.D.: Born and brought up in Fort William, he was a native Gaelic speaker and a distinguished medical graduate, who held the posts of consultant physician and surgeon and medical superintendent at the Belford Hospital, Fort William, for 41 years. He had a massive knowledge and first-hand experience of existing services throughout the West Highlands.

Dr John L. Robertson M.A., LLB. C.B.: Furnished with an impressive CV in the arts and the law, Robertson held an honorary doctorate from Edinburgh University. He was a native of Stornoway, Isle of Lewis, and at the time of his appointment to the committee was the Senior Chief Inspector of Schools for Scotland.

The Marchioness of Tullibardine (née Ramsay): Kitty Ramsay, or Kitty Tullibardine, was a lively addition to the Committee and, like many ladies of her station, had a first-class record of public service. She was married into the mighty Murray of Atholl family and was a Unionist politician of her day. She was also a trained musician of professional standard.

THE DEWAR COMMITTEE

The committee was appointed by the Treasury in 1912 to enquire into the provision of medical attendance in the Highlands and Islands of Scotland. It was distinguished in its membership as well as in its chairman, Sir John Dewar, then MP for Inverness-shire, and the eponymous scion of the Scotch Whisky distillers based in Perth. True to its specific remit outlined at p. 43, evidence was gathered and a report was prepared, all within the year of 1912. In 1913 the report was formally presented to both Houses of Parliament. Astonishingly, this particular H.M. Treasury Report was not placed on some shelf to gather dust: it was acted on at once.

In regard to the taking of evidence, questionnaires were sent to local doctors and 158 other persons, an itinerary of meetings was arranged, visiting all those communities in the Highlands and Islands included in their schedule. In addition, they held other meetings in Edinburgh and Glasgow, and reviewed available published reports and papers. In essence, it was a pretty thorough and efficient exercise. Dr Lachlan Grant gave evidence to the committee in Oban on 28 October 1912. (For a transcript of Dr Grant's evidence, see Appendix III.) This was in a two-part presentation of 'question and answer' and a separate written submission. In detail presented, interesting facts were noted. His overall list of patients in 1912 amounted to 3500 patients, 1200 of whom were Kinlochleven-based. Though he carried overall responsibility of care for such a vast number of people, he did engage an assistant resident doctor at Kinlochleven.

As to means of transport, he confirmed this to be by motor car, bicycle, walking, motor boat, rowing boat, steamer and train. In this context, one notes the Callander & Oban Railway opened its spur branch from Connel to Ballachulish in 1903, greatly improving access. The motor car cost him £60 per year to operate and pre-motor car he owned a horse. This was quite a common mode of transport over the Highlands and Islands terrain in those days, and most effective. In a fascinating encounter with the committee, Dr Grant gave account of establishing a bacteriology laboratory at his surgery premises and of the great value it was in the care of his patients, especially in regard to the early diagnosis of TB by way of microscopic examination of sputum. This service he extended to other GP colleagues and, in the interests of public health, was also made available throughout the county of Argyll. Vaccination programmes were an important and significant activity as a means of controlling the blight of the prevalent infections of the times.

On matters of general practice finance, and the current payment arrangements, there was much to be corrected. In his own case, he revealed that in Ballachulish there existed the 'Club', towards which the workmen paid 3½ pence per week or 15s 2d per year. This covered medical care of the workman and his family and the same charge was applied to single men. For maternity and vaccination services there was a separate charge. The club operated at Ballachulish Quarry where he had 200 men on the register and at Kentallen Quarry where 40 men were registered. A secretary and treasurer collected the money from each pay and administered the arrangement of reward. By 1912 the club system of payment had been in effect for some 50 years.

Overall Dr Grant listed his duties as:

Parish Medical Officer.
Local MOH.
Medical Officer of the Fever Hospital.
Medical Officer to the Workmen's Medical Society.
Consulting Medical Officer to B.A. Co., Kinlochleven works.
Certifying Factory Surgeon.
Bacteriologist to Lorn, Ardnamurchan and Mull districts of the County Council.

It paints a picture of a truly busy professional man, then in his early 40s. The laboratory work was a personal interest of Dr Grant's and, along with his optical services providing lenses to his patients, which he had performed since 1904, reflected his undoubted skill in those particular fields.

Summarising his main suggestions to the committee, Dr Grant stated; 'First and foremost comes adequate remuneration, then relief from uncertainty and useless competition and a reasonable amount of leisure. I have given the problem considerable thought and confess I have no adequate solution along the old lines of general practice. We require a new departure in the form of a full state medical service for our Highlands and Islands.'

While all the doctors and witnesses before the committee gave a very good account of themselves, and graphically described the problems, many observers, then and since, noted something unique about the presentation made by Dr Grant. What they noted was this: while all others brought the problems, Dr Lachlan Grant brought the solutions. It was to his everlasting credit that the committee, when it made its recommendations to the government, endorsed all of Dr Grant's suggestions in its report.

As a result of the Dewar Committee's report, the government of the day set up, in 1913, the Highlands and Islands Medical Service (HIMS) with a Treasury grant of £42,000. Doctors were given a basic income and could continue to treat private patients. Fees were set at a minimal level. Inability to pay did not prevent people getting treatment. State resources were directed to

15 Highlands and Islands Medical Service Committee

October

21st to 22nd

Highlands & Islands Medical Service Committee.

Katharine Tullibardine

John Cameron

J. G. Grierson

A. C. Miller.

W. Leslie Mackenzie.

M. Pearson. Secy.

Nov. 30th to Dec 1st

Andrew Lindsay

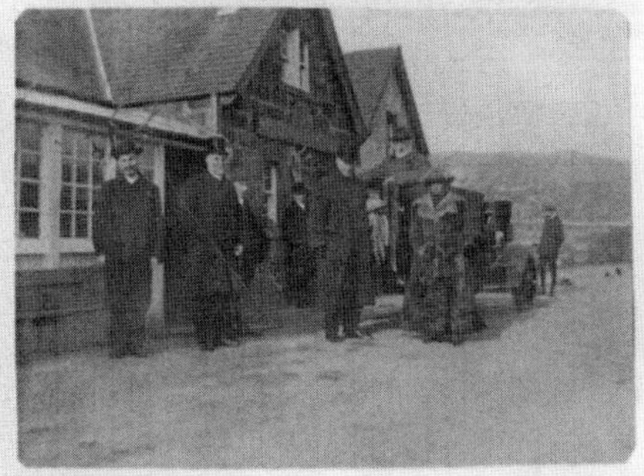

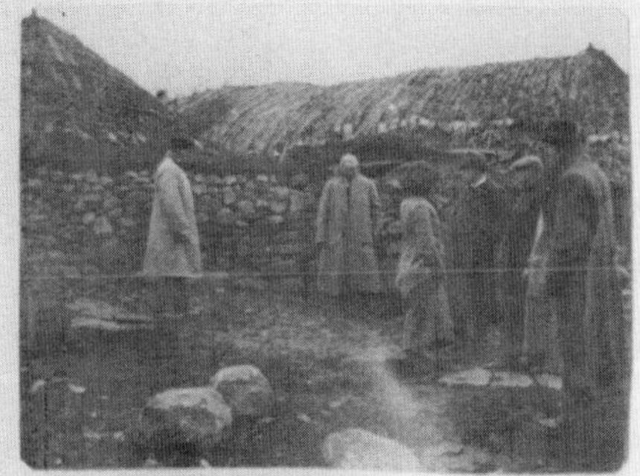

16 Highlands and Islands
Medical Service Committee

Top left: The Hotel,
Rhiconnich, 16 October
1912

Top right: Crossing The
Minch

Bottom left: Stornoway,
11 and 12 October 1912

Bottom right: A visit to
Callanish, Isle of Lewis,
12 October 1912

basic needs – providing a house, telephone, car or motorboat to get around, and cover for study leave and holiday.

Outbreak of World War 1 did delay introduction of the service, and real progress in terms of coverage did not materialise until hostilities ended in 1919. However, there was satisfaction that in 1914 St Kilda had acquired its first resident nurse. Eventually progress was made, and by 1929 there were 175 nurses and 160 doctors in 150 practices throughout the Highlands and Islands. It was hailed as a 'unique social experiment in Britain'; it was directly funded by the state, and centrally administered by the Scottish Office in Edinburgh, working with local committees. HIMS revolutionised medical care for more than 300,000 people living on half the land mass of Scotland. It was an outstanding success, universally acclaimed. By the year of 1945 it had delivered 25 years of comprehensive care, and rightly deserved to become the prototype for the National Health Service itself, founded as it was in the United Kingdom in 1948.

Of all the campaigns he led and fronted, and the social reforms he fought for, it is an undeniable fact that the hard won improvements in health care in the Highlands, and the advent of a National Health Service in the country, proved to be Dr Grant's greatest triumph, and the one he was most closely associated with as an early pioneer. It was, historically, a shame that the intervention of the First World War interrupted and interfered with the rolling out of the HIMS programme, and slowed its progress for a while. Throughout its years of toil, however, it struck a record to be proud of, and attracted no little admiration. Dr Grant would be the first to testify to such a fact, and propose a toast to such success.

A NATIONAL HEALTH SERVICE

Among Dr Grant's personal collection of papers, articles, journals and other material, are many documents of interest and historical relevance. Of his many written compositions on the health service of his day, the following essay is one of special importance and serves to demonstrate for us the innate social reformer he truly was, back in those distant days. It is evident he was ahead of his time and it is also clear he was a visionary. Like a diamond set in a ring, the article deserves to see the light of day once more and be sported for us all to admire, for its own intrinsic worth.

A National Health Service

Lachlan Grant

Whatever the faults of the National Health Insurance Act maybe, it must be admitted that it has given a very great impetus to the idea of an efficient national medical service; and it is certain that a much more comprehensive scheme will be in operation before many years.

The advantages of a consolidation of all the present medical and nursing activities are apparent; and that, reinforced by adequate equipment and further specialisation in every branch, would give the country the maximum of prevention at the minimum of expense.

Every individual and every section of the community would benefit by an organised network of health preservation and disease prevention machinery; and just as every corner in the land is served by the post office and the police controlled by a central authority, so would the 'Scottish' Ministry of Health's organisation penetrate to every house and hamlet from John o' Groats to the Mull of Galloway. But no class would benefit more than the womenfolk, especially the mothers in rural or outlandish districts. In some parts they only see a doctor once in several months, and some mothers with large families have never had medical attendance or skilled nursing. Many cases of hardship could be related, and although some efforts have been made to cope with these under present conditions, it is obvious to all who know the facts that nothing short of a government health preservation system will suffice to fully meet them. Some sections of the country are so poor and difficult to work and would never pay a medical man depending largely on fees; and it is with many doctors much of their hard work is given ungrudgingly without, or with very inadequate, remuneration. They are handicapped, and are prevented giving their patients of the best that modern medicine knows as they are unable to efficiently equip – keep their appointments and keep themselves up to date. The excellent work of the Highlands and Islands Medical Service Committee is only one example of effort which could be more generally applied in a 'free' Scotland.

What is wanted is a national system of public health that will provide:-
1 Medical Attendance
2 Nursing and ambulance services
3 Modern medical and surgical hospital accommodation
4 Houses for maternity cases and convalescents
5 Popular education in health hygiene, first-aid, and simple remedies.

Every parent, and especially every mother, ought to be so far enlightened in matters of health that dangers due to lack of knowledge would be obviated. There will doubtless be a special propaganda department under the new regime and advice and guidance in the form of pamphlets will be conveyed to all and sundry. The aim would be to inculcate principles from childhood upwards that would prevent wrong habits and other conditions that make for disease and premature mortality.

Mother, in the most important sense, is the real head of the household, and she would be regarded as a sort of sub-officer of public health in close alliance with such an established state service. It is short-sighted policy that would deny mothers and children the best that medicine and trained nursing can provide because they happen to be in poor circumstances or living in the country's outskirts. If patriotism rise to the occasion it will see that, at any cost, the mothers and children, at least, will want for nothing that makes for the best and highest health and efficiency.

All this the coming national service will secure; and some of the results will be a lessened infantile death rate, a large reduction in the ratio of children's diseases, more efficient school work and better school attendance, a lessened average of workers' absence through illness, a decrease in troubles such as nervous breakdowns, fever cases for hospitals, infirmaries, asylums, and prisons and a lower rate of mortality among the over-burdened and poorer class of mothers. Instead of the nurse and the doctor being avoided on the ground of expense and only called in at the eleventh hour, they would be immediately apprised of the approach of danger and prompt measures against the enemy would be the order of the day.

If every person had to consider individual payment of fees before calling for the protection of law and police there would be much more crime to deal with; but the law of the land and the police being a national and social matter, every citizen feels a personal interest in combating crime – which is only another form of disease – and works in alliance with the forces of law and order.

Some critics may say that under such a paternal system people would flock wholesale to the doctors and constantly worry them with unnecessary calls; but this would right itself in time, and it would be better to have everybody reporting themselves with their more or less imaginary complaints and discover the dangerous cases than that they should hold themselves back and allow infection and disease to spread unchecked. In due time people would be so far enlightened that their imaginary ailments would become a very small quantity and the work of hygienic education and prevention would eventually eliminate the merely stupid notions of the ignorant and the idle fancies of the supersensitive.

The improved health equipment placed at the disposal of the mothers and the nations would alone repay the entire cost of such a national medical service.

The constant patrol of the police of public health – or the 'missionaries of public welfare' as they might aptly be termed – guarding our homes from the insidious enemies that cause needless suffering and deterioration would eliminate a vast amount of material loss. And what is even of greater importance, would dissipate much of the mental depression and moral apathy that weigh so heavily upon many of the people."

The entire article was published in *The Free Man – a Journal of Independent Thought,* volume III, no.2 on Saturday, February 10, 1934, and on his own personal copy of the article, Dr Grant in a hand-written note, had endorsed it: 'the above = a re-written article. LG.' It is of great interest that the article contained the seeds he himself had sown in his evidence to the Dewar Committee in 1912, that the original article itself was composed some time after the HIMS had set about delivering its health plan for the Highlands and Islands (which he refers to) and, of course, this reprinted version surfaced in publication in 1934. Clearly, there was no letting up on his part in striving for a national health service, and one senses that he in fact believed this to be an inevitable outcome. The National Health Service did materialise, but not until 1948, too late for Dr Grant to be its cheerleader.

LAND REFORM AND THE 'HIGHLAND PROBLEMS'

Not one to rest on his laurels, or rest at all, after the First World War ended Dr Grant turned his attention to land reform issues and 'the Highland problems.' He wrote reams in the press and spoke volubly in public on these subjects and solutions to them. In 1933 he and his true soul-mate, the Rev Thomas Murchison of Glenelg, joined forces with Compton MacKenzie and John Lorne Campbell of Canna, to establish the Sea League (see overleaf): to defend the West Coast fishing industry and the livelihood of the inshore fishermen on the west coast, and to press the case with the government for legal protection from the powerful and rapacious east coast and southern-based trawlers. Branches were formed in the Western Isles, the west mainland, and even the Highland towns. The Sea League battled long and hard with the Westminster politicians and the Edinburgh civil servants to achieve any measure of success.

THE SEA LEAGUE

When Compton MacKenzie and John Lorne Campbell first mooted the Sea League in Barra in 1933, they produced a leaflet in Gaelic and English which they distributed around the island, and, in due course of time, much further afield, as the League gained support. MacKenzie was the chairman and Campbell the secretary. Dr Lachlan Grant and the Rev Thomas Murchison were to join them soon after the Sea League was formed.

The information disseminated in the leaflet read as follows:

'WHAT THE SEA LEAGUE STANDS FOR
The Sea League has been formed to demand the same protection for the livelihood of the crofter fisherman as is given to the sporting fishing of the landowners themselves.

Barra, Outer Hebrides 20th December 1933: objects of the League are:

That the Minch, between a line from Barra Head to Tiree and a line from the Butt of Lewis to Cape Wrath, shall be closed to trawlers and that the fishing in this area shall be regulated for the benefit of the fishermen who live around it.

That the penalties for illegal trawling shall be increased and the policing of the inshore waters made more efficient.

That the fines for illegal trawling shall be used for financing fishermen who have lost their gear through illegal trawling, or who want to commence inshore fishing for the first time.

The Sea League intends to fight unceasingly for these objects.

JOIN THE SEA LEAGUE. Subscription, one shilling. Write (in Gaelic or English) to The Secretary, Northbay, Barra.'

The well-organised and rehearsed flurry of activity from 1930 onwards was all with serious political purpose in mind. From Highland Society ceilidh platforms in Glasgow and elsewhere, Dr Grant delivered his 'big speeches,' spelling out the problems, setting out their extent, and fleshing out answers. At a Clan MacColl Society meeting in the Highlanders' Institute, Glasgow, one evening, he roundly condemned emigration and the fact that the Highlanders had never had the justice and fair play which the Irish and colonial interests had obtained.

Loss of our people through emigration had got us into a much poorer state and was, in itself, a 'process of national and racial suicide.' Fundamental reconstruction of the Highlands had to take place, and above all else there had to be a land settlement policy to arrest the dreary decline. 'Our heritage is in danger,' he warned, 'and the development of agriculture, forestry, tweed-making, fisheries, the slate quarries, and new industries dependent on water power have to take shape.' Unless the country 'woke up,' he sensed, the best method of coping with the problems of the Highlands would be by way and means of a Scottish Parliament. On this occasion, Dr Grant had taken his 'prisoner.' In the best stage-managed fashion, he had earlier secured the Prime Minister's offer of support and backing for his plan. So, the letter received from Ramsay MacDonald was read aloud to the meeting:

'Not only Glasgow, but England, and the Dominions overseas, have drawn from our Highland districts thousands of their best people as emigrants. Too little was done in the past to make it possible for the Highlander to remain at home and to enjoy within his native shores the full opportunities of life. We are now fully alive to the needs of the Highlands and Islands. Much has been done by way of sharing the land more equally, helping the people to improve their houses, supplying adequate schools and medical services, and easing the difficulties of communication. But much remains to be done, and any well-advised schemes for the social, economic and cultural benefit of the Highlands will be received by me with the warmest of sympathy.'

But Dr Grant was not to be so easily placated and he did not lower his sights. The main task to be tackled was the reconstruction of the whole Highlands and one of the most important problems was the land question. 'Without land,' he claimed, 'there will be no existence.' At every opportunity and at every public rally he was to address, Lachlan Grant was to hammer home his message: 'Highlanders have never had justice and fair play because they have been without leaders and without a voice, or vocal ones, in the councils of rulers.' It would have been a much better plan, he declared, to have kept the tillers on the soil and given them a right and title to it and a patent to nourish it, replenish it, and swell its bounty. The policy of emigration, by its very nature, was an evil one. The clearances and evictions were crimes for which the whole nation, not isolated landlords, was responsible. His own response was the adoption of a 'wise, paternal policy, calculated to re-people the hills and straths, to galvanise the scattered centres of Highland population in activity.' The passion on display as he propounded his plans for reforms and social justice was as impressive as it was sincere. He also demonstrated well-honed political skills, and of course he was very accomplished as an author and speech-writer.

From early 1930 to December 1934, Dr Grant was never silent on these matters of great concern to him. The effort expended had everything to do with preparing people for the publication of his pamphlet, *A New Deal for the Highlands,* * which he produced in December 1934 to press and public acclaim. The publication brought together all the earlier themes and locked them into the one text. Once the plan was rolled out, the next path to pave was the launching of 'the League,' or 'the Highland Development League,' which Dr Grant and Rev Thomas Murchison founded at a well-attended public meeting in Glasgow in January 1936. It was a business-like organisation with a full legal constitution and appointed office-bearers. Dr Lachlan Grant was elected chairman, Dr Alexander Nisbet, Glasgow, and Rev Thomas Murchison were elected vice-chairmen and the elected clerk and treasurer was Mr Donald MacKay, a solicitor in the firm Downie Aitken & Co., Glasgow.

Along with the Land Settlement Association, the Highland Development League set about the founding of branches far and wide, e.g. in Portree, Glasgow, Edinburgh, Carlisle, Oban, Callander, Kinlochleven, Ross-shire, London, Inverness, Campbeltown, Cullipool and Toberonachy – a truly impressive spread of activity. The purpose of the League was to recruit as many members and supporters as possible who would go on to explain and expound the concepts embraced in the 'New Deal' and the plan for action to be pursued with the political class.

The New Deal had to address the special problems wholeheartedly and make its impact throughout the Highland land mass. At the start it boldly laid down its assertion that 'the sum of one million pounds for thirty years, spent in the Highlands for purposes of land settlement and development alone, would be an inadequate return to the race for the sacrifice of blood and spirit in the

---

* In his publication, *New Deal for the Highlands*, Dr Grant framed five objectives:

Teaching of agricultural subjects in all schools under qualified instructors.
Lectures to farmers in agri-centres.
Instruction by films and other demonstrations.
A national land system giving security of tenure, minimum rent charges, and the help of the government in developing agriculture.
Land reclamation of ground once fertile but now lying fallow.

His calculation was that at least £1million a year for 30 years had to be spent in the Highlands for purposes of land settlement and development alone, to make any impression.

interest of the British Commonwealth of Nations.'

Claim was also made that a Scottish Parliament would be a great advance and pave the way for far-reaching changes throughout Scotland. The New Deal contemplated special separate treatment for the Highlands and the necessity of a Grand Committee of the Scottish Parliament to deal entirely with Highland questions. Dr Grant himself had, by this time, lost a good deal of patience and faith with the London-based Government and had made his position plain: 'The advent of a Scottish legislature would stimulate the whole Scottish people and awake interest in our problems and the greater problem of civilisation. It would be a great lever for raising the general conditions of life and for making the Highlands and Islands what they ought to be – model communities, inhabited by a prosperous, healthy and contented people.'

In all of this, and in the wider political context, Dr Grant's political views did not in any way deviate from those of Highland Liberalism. Indeed, at this stage, he was singing from the same hymn sheet as Johnnie Bannerman and, what is more, he was actively canvassing for Bannerman around 1938 in the Argyll constituency. Home Rule was an issue to rally round, one that united them. However, soon there were cracks developing. When in 1937/38 it came to the next passionate political campaign, over the Caledonian Power Scheme, the role and behaviour of the London Parliament was one Grant found hard to take. The Power Bill led to much controversy and division along the lines of the Highland scenery versus the potential of new Highland industries powered by hydro-electricity. To crown it all, the Caledonian Power Scheme Bill was rejected despite its approval by Scottish MPs at Westminster by a majority of 4 to 1. The issue so incensed Dr Grant that in April 1937 he took himself onto a public platform in Kinlochleven village and fiercely fought back: 'If we had a few more healthy communities like Kinlochleven in the Highlands and Islands, we would have advanced considerably towards a solution of the Highland problems. Those people who level criticism are often those who do not earn their bread and butter in the Highland area.' In one final salvo, he declared: 'It sets us furiously to think that fact compels every thinking Scottish man and woman to consider the merit of Scottish Government.'

Of course one must not forget that 1936 had thrown up an interesting political interlude. In the Ross and Cromarty parliamentary constituency a by-election had been triggered by the elevation of Sir Ian MacPherson, the National Liberal MP, to the peerage. Then, as now, the political thicket was full of intrigue. A cabinet minister by the name of Malcolm MacDonald, the son of Ramsay MacDonald, had just been narrowly beaten in his Bassetlaw seat at the General Election in 1935 and was eagerly looking for a new seat. The National Liberal Association was the dominant Liberal faction in the Ross and Cromarty constituency. They approached MacDonald to stand as the National Government candidate for the seat. He agreed. The manoeuvre upset the Unionists who had previously supported Sir Ian MacPherson and they invited Randolph Churchill, the son of Winston Churchill, to be their candidate. He was adopted by 160 votes to 47. In turn the Scottish Liberal Federation representing the Liberal Party, were incensed that an ex-Labour politician (MacDonald) had been adopted and they were determined to contest the seat. Political intrigue flourished.

Liberals throughout the Highlands were at pains to attract a home-grown figure of credibility and charisma, such as Lachlan Grant. They set out to woo him and persuade him to accept nomination as the Liberal candidate. There was no doubt he had all the right arrows in his political quiver. He had over the years built up a massive reputation and his leading role in the Crofters' and Cottars' Association and the Sea League and his recently published 'New Deal' had won him many plaudits. The Liberals did their utmost to persuade him to stand on their behalf. They beseeched him for weeks. But when the decision was finally made it was a polite refusal and the Liberal baton passed to a total outsider. They adopted Dr W.S. Russell Thomas, a complete no-hoper, as their candidate. Labour, in the meantime, were to adopt Mr Hector MacNeill, a Glasgow councillor, who had missed winning Kelvingrove at the recent General Election, and the Scottish National Party decided not to contest the seat.

The by-election was held on 10 February 1936 after a hectic campaign fought in the midst of a Highland winter. The only dash of colour to be injected into the contest, it seems, was Randolph Churchill's bright scarlet waistcoat, viewed as he stood on Dingwall's railway platform. But, more seriously, enormous national publicity was generated by the campaign, which was interrupted and suspended for several days following the death of King George V, resuming after his funeral. MacDonald won the election. As the National Government candidate he won the seat by a majority of 2,982 votes over Labour's Hector MacNeill. Churchill gained a modest third place with 13.4% of the vote and the Liberals were bottom of the poll with a mere 738 votes.

It remains a mystery why such a politically active operator on the Highland scene as Dr Grant declined an opportunity to fight the Ross-shire seat. He had the Highland political tide running in his favour; he had Ross-shire roots; he was a Gael to the marrow and a professional man to his fingertips. His contribution to Highland affairs was unmatched and his reputation as champion of the Highlands was without equal. Great was the speculation that ensued! True, Dr Grant was then 65 years of age, not the best time in life to embark on a Westminster career. It was also the case that he was increasingly disenchanted with London-based governments. Also not to be discounted, of course, was the potential embarrassment of standing against his best friend's son and scuppering MacDonald's political career by defeating him. In all fairness, there was no doubting Malcolm MacDonald was a most able, honest and honourable man who well deserved membership of Parliament. Yet the question remains, what might have been?

As stated earlier, the by-election was an interlude. Once over, wider Highland and political battles resumed, to be fought in hand to hand fashion. The issues and debates were brought into still sharper focus and the cry for action became ever more pressing. Campaigners found the lethargy and inertia, so typical of government, impossible to comprehend. Patience was wearing thin and little or nothing was being achieved. It cried out for new answers.

THE BACTERIOLOGICAL LABORATORIES, BALLACHULISH

Dr Grant firmly believed that the earlier the diagnosis, the better the outcome for the patient. To this end he was also of the opinion that the most modern methods available should be employed by doctors to assist in the accurate diagnosis of any ailment. Research he saw as an on-going thing and he was a frequent contributor to medical journals on various aspects of pathology and immunology.

From early days in general practice at Ballachulish, Dr Grant had equipped the practice with laboratory facilities, albeit of a basic standard initially. When he built his new medical facility at West Laroch in 1929, the medical pavilion (an integral part of Craigleven) was planned to house an up-to-date, modern laboratory. So enthused by the experience must he have been that he wrote and published a pamphlet detailing 'How to equip a modern bacteriological laboratory'. Within this laboratory Dr Grant had to hand the necessary equipment to facilitate diagnosis. Even more remarkably, it contained many items of equipment that he himself had invented. Microscopic work was paramount: examination of stool, sputum and urine samples, as well as wound swabs, was undertaken. Typhoid, and in later years, tuberculosis were major diseases to test for and identify. On such activity Dr Grant published annual data in the form of pathology laboratory tables, which explained such clinical activity.

Dr Grant's Bacteriological Report for 1932 was typical of the presentation made and was compiled as follows:

Bacteriology Report 1932

The Bacteriological Laboratories
Ballachulish

Mortality table giving the death rate per 1,000 of the
estimated population from all forms of tuberculosis

	Pulmonary TB	Non-Pulmonary TB	All TB
No. of Deaths	36	19	55
Death rate	0.58	0.31	0.89

During the past year over 500 specimens were received at the laboratory.
The bulk of these samples were from patients suspected of having tuberculosis disease of the lungs or from patients having suspicious and
indefinite throat infections, and thought to be suffering from diphtheria.
Specimen from the other rarer illnesses, such as infections from the
typhoid group of micro-organisms also came to hand, as well as many
samples of septic discharges, pus, etc., for identification.

Dr Lachlan Grant M.D.

17 The Bacteriological Laboratory at Craigleven

Inventions and Creations

Lachlan Grant had a penchant for creating things and one can sense he was strongly of the view that necessity was indeed the mother of invention. In his early days as a GP he would certainly be aware of the lack of tools available to any doctor in the execution of medical duties and procedures and the limitations such a situation imposed. Perhaps it also had to do with the tradition in his father's family for designing and drawing, from scratch, new inventions and gadgets, and for modifying others. In this context it is of interest to study the advert card published and circulated by 'Grant & McFarlane' to proclaim the arrival of an upgraded model of one of their manufactured goods – the 'Improved Washing Machine.' Dr Grant had a list of 'creations' to his credit, some of which he brought to public notice, and not all of relevance to medicine. Many were intended for domestic or social purposes.

THE GRANT TEAPOT
The most notable creation, one that progressed to production, was the 'Grant Teapot.' This plain practical utensil was intended to enhance the whole expe-

18 The Grant Teapot

rience of tea-making. It comprised a standard-looking glazed clay teapot with an aluminium metal paddle attached to its lid, which could be turned via its wooden lid holder. The paddle action enabled the infused tea to be uniformly and evenly stirred, the tea leaves remaining undisturbed by the action. The item bore the Patent No.122093 and, in its mint state still, the prototype has been passed to the care of Dr Macleod at Craigleven, thanks to the kindness of Mrs Roddan and her family.

SUNSHADES

The light aluminium framed sunshades created by Dr Grant are marvellously simple and practical. Of course one should not forget that he was as good as expert on eye matters. Thus the invention itself he based on simple observation. In an everyday situation, when the sun shines brightly and one focuses to the distance, one raises a hand horizontally across one's brow, so creating a 'shade,' or enough darkness to permit the pupil of the eyes more flexibility in dilating. This gives better accommodation and thereby optimum light conditions to see with. The shades comprised light aluminium frames which clipped round the ears and sported circular rims, without any lens, to which hooded metal awnings were attached at eyebrow level. The old photographs of a local villager demonstrating the use of the shades, and the ophthalmic principle at play, while standing outside Dr Grant's garden shed and gazing into the sunlight are a real treasure!

THE PORTABLE RESERVOIR WITH SPRAY

On the medical front, the 'Portable Reservoir with Spray' well deserves mention. It was essentially a practical piece of equipment, designed to minimise the risk of infection and cross-infection. In those days of yore such a problem was of even greater concern than it is today. This apparatus is the most famous of his inventions. It was a device he was personally invited to lecture on and to demonstrate to medical colleagues and audiences at Royal Colleges, universities, hospitals and clinics. What is even more gratifying is that it received good coverage in the *British Medical Journal*, in the issue of 18 November 1939. In the publication Dr Grant declared he had been experimenting with 'an apparatus designed to afford in the patient's home, at the bedside, an aseptic wash comparable to that obtained at the elevated spray faucet of an operating theatre.' He described it as consisting of 'a light rectangular-sided tank 20 inches long, 8 inches broad, and 12 inches deep, made of stainless steel or of vitreous enamelled metal, so rendering it more impervious to most corrosive lotions.'

The tank weighed about 10lbs and had the capacity of four gallons. An opening in the upper surface was large enough to admit one's hand for cleaning the tank and was used for filling purposes. The opening was sealed off with an easy-fitting cap. A draw-off tap with a spray outlet was fitted to the reservoir and the tap operated by means of an aluminium lever handle which was easily detached and controlled, when in use, by the elbow. There was also an optional type of tap that could be fitted – an all-metal one with a hinged one-way joint. The tap was operated by raising or lowering the nozzle, as required. Flow from both taps was by gravity only. The apparatus could fit into a case about the size of a midwifery bag and be easily carried to the patient's bedside.

'For use,' Dr Grant explained, 'the tank should be filled with pure water at any suitable temperature. This may be done direct from a kettle or ewer. If a lotion is being employed, this should be poured from a jug or may even be mixed in the reservoir. The cap having been replaced, the tank should then be elevated, to ensure the necessary gravity flow from the spray, by placing it on a small table or other support – a fairly large round or oval basin should be placed below the spray to collect the waste.' He claimed the apparatus was light, compact and easily transportable by hand, cycle or car. He argued that

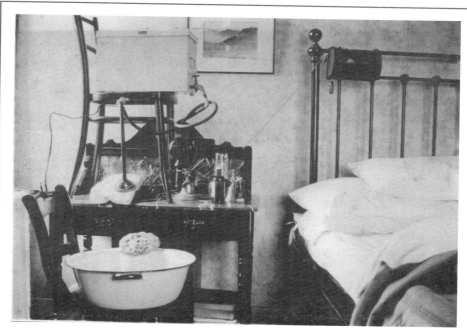

19 Portable Reservoir with Spray

it obviated the risk that always accompanies washing in still water, or lotion, in a basin. The hands, or swabs, could be cleansed under a running supply of uncontaminated water and antiseptic lotion at the bedside. 'The water or lotion in the tank keeps warmer for a longer time and is less liable to aerial floral contamination than is the case with water or lotion lying exposed in an open basin,' Dr Grant explained. He maintained that by washing under running water, any gross or septic material from the skin surfaces flowed away and organisms were thus not reapplied to the cleansed surfaces. In his enthusiasm, Dr Grant maintained, 'An aseptic or antiseptic wash can be achieved with minimum expenditure or fluid. This is also an advantage where water is scarce, in areas with low annual rainfalls or in other special circumstances.' Such a statement would hardly apply to the west coast of Scotland! However, Dr Grant was firmly of the view that the reservoir should be part of the armamentarium of any practitioner engaged in domiciliary midwifery or surgery, whether or not water was laid on in the houses being attended. He also highlighted its attractiveness to veterinary surgeons, and to nurses in the course of their work. It was possible to install it in motor and air ambulances where surgical or obstetrical emergencies may have to be dealt with and should be part of the equipment of all first-aid posts. Likewise, its usefulness in field dressing and casualty stations should be obvious, he said, and its advantage to practitioners in the tropics and aboard ship should be appreciated on account of its economy of water.

The equipment was made for Dr Grant by Messrs. Archibald Young and Sons Ltd., of Forrest Road, Edinburgh. He advertised his wares accordingly but no information is available as to how successful the orders and sales became. It is certain though that Dr Grant possessed one, that he put it to good use and that he was the proud father to its invention!

THE ALUMINIUM THROAT SWABS

Undoubtedly Dr Grant was proud of the 'new metal' that was aluminium, the very product manufactured within his practice area, and he was alive to its advantages and natural qualities in the making of other products and devices. In this regard, he and his assistant, Dr William Murdie, were in 1913 to come forward with the idea of an 'improved throat swab made from aluminium wire.' Both inventors made specific claims for it.

The ordinary types of swabs then in use had several serious drawbacks and the view was that a more efficient instrument had to be devised. Swabs made of copper, iron, steel or thin nickel wire were easily tarnished and, if left lying in a climate of the least damp, were liable to become discoloured and unsuitable for use. Copper and nickel were apt to develop verdigris from soluble copper and nickel salts, and brown discolouration was likely to happen with those made of iron, which developed rust or ferrous oxide. Quite reasonably it was stated that such swabs, if used, or laid aside for a time, acquired an unattractive and unhygienic appearance and were not the sort of thing to ask a patient to admit to his throat. The pledget of sterile wool was also likely to be stained, and as the soluble copper nickel salts were germicidal, these swabs could more or less invalidate the bacterial diagnosis.

By the use of the aluminium wire, Dr Grant insisted, these and 'other undesirable accompaniments' could be obviated. The wire was easily moulded to shape and yet rigid enough for swabbing purposes; and it kept bright and clean. It seemed an aluminium swab never became soiled or discoloured in appearance like these other metals. Moreover it stood boiling well, was easy to clean and redress and did not contain any bactericidal element. In design, the aluminium swab had a safety ring which avoided the need to hold the swab by its cork plug end. This afforded complete control over movements of the swab and thus minimised the risk of introducing organisms other than a patient's own. As there was no fear of 'rusting' or 'greening', the cotton pledget could be held under a running tap before swabbing a patient's throat, ensuring a good sample of the infected secretion, and also retarding the drying effects of transmission through the post.

Being the renowned bacteriologist that he was, Dr Grant was forever at pains to stress the diagnostic and prognostic value of swab-taking and he maintained that the throat swab was an essential item in the practitioner's tool kit. 'We know,' he said, 'it is practically impossible without a bacteriological examination to make sure whether a patient who complains of a sore throat is suffering from diphtheria, mixed-throat infection, Vincent's angina, follicular tonsillitis, or an infection of the Treponema pallidum.' It was his firm belief that tests thoroughly carried out from start to finish were invaluable in speedily determining or eliminating certain or all of these diseases, and so removed the anxiety attached to an undecided clinical diagnosis. Thus to attain that, a hygienic, safe, clean, light, and easily handled swab was an important adjunct!

The aluminium throat swab was a useful and practical improvement, one Dr Grant himself put to daily use in his medical work in his own bacteriological laboratory at Ballachulish.

7

Promotion of Industry, Work and Welfare

When Peter Grant, his wife and young family arrived in the glen in 1880, with his sister Ann Barr, to establish the grocery business of Barr & Co., they were settling into a community that was economically based and dependent on an old-established industry. Slate quarrying in Ballachulish spoke of history that dated back to within one year of the Massacre of Glencoe. Quarrying was an industry, in every sense of the term, and the humble village gained a national reputation for roofing Scottish towns and cities. In this respect the Argyllshire village was quite unlike most parts of the Highlands and Islands where local work and employment were hard to come by at that time. The rural economy in the northern counties was not then in good heart.

In 1880 the slate industry employed 600 men and was therefore a major employer in North Lorn. The market, though, was noted for its ups and downs, and the volatility, in combination with poor wages and conditions, did not make for stable and agreeable employment.

When Dr Grant arrived to take up his appointment as medical officer to the quarries company in August 1900, the workforce was then down to about 400 men. Grant's early years in post (and out of it) taught him many worthwhile lessons, which evidently shaped his views on such important issues as the need for work, employment and better working conditions for workers. As a doctor, he was also well aware of the impact these matters had on homes and communities as a whole. From his early days in the Highlands, therefore, it became a mission to do all in his power to promote industry and create well-paid jobs so as to improve people's welfare generally and raise morale in communities like his own.

Mrs Roddan, Dr Grant's only surviving daughter, says she cannot remember a time when her father was not actively involved in pursuing the means by which to 'promote jobs for Highland people.' Indeed one can easily audit this. In some ways, in the early days, his prayers seemed to be answered. Transport and communications received a big boost in his county when the Callander & Oban Railway line was extended from Connel to Ballachulish, between 1901 and 1903. Though the building of the line was physically hard, with no mechanical machinery on site (it was all pick and shovel), there was an opportunity for local labour to be recruited on the project. Nonetheless, of the large workforce engaged, some 3,000 men, most were an influx of itinerant navvies from all over the country and from Ireland. Once constructed, the railway served the area well by improving transport facilities and aiding trade. It was an opportune time and became more so thanks to the prospect of a totally new industry proposed for construction at the head of Loch Leven, at the isolated farm settlements of Kinlochbeg and Kinlochmore. Plans for a major aluminium smelter, a hydro-electric power scheme to supply it, and an entire new village built to accommodate the workforce had been mooted since 1895 but abandoned through the opposition of the landlords. By 1904, however, the necessary Bills had been passed and obstacles had been removed. The following year the engineering work on this massive project was in full swing, with a rapid build-up of the workforce. In this matter Dr Grant found himself to be the occupational health doctor, an awesome clinical task.

The concept, as well as the project, had the support and blessing of Dr Grant from its earliest days. He formed a very comfortable relationship with the heads of the British Alcan Company, who controlled the project, and he gave them a good deal of support in their aims. Grant saw the entire scheme as a dream about to come true: a major employer, good wages to be paid and regular steady employment. For local men and their families it presented a golden opportunity and afforded a means whereby one empty Highland glen, at least, would be re-populated. Dr Lachlan Grant was extremely proud of what was being created at Kinlochleven and he never lost an opportunity of promoting it. The 'City among the Hills,' he lovingly labelled Kinlochleven and that 'city' has never had a more passionate advocate than he. The villages of Foyers and Kinlochleven he looked on as glowing examples of what could be achieved for the Highlands and Islands of Scotland. The scale, nature and impact of such developments also aroused his awareness and alerted him to the potential of a New World opening up through the generation of electricity by harnessing hydropower. Hydro schemes, so designed and built, he saw as being sympathetic to isolated rural communities as well as being good sources of employment in areas of the far north much in need of it.

On a much more minor scale, locally, Dr Grant was to welcome the development of sea transport from Ballachulish to Kinlochleven for freight and passengers. In 1905 his own brother John launched the service with his 25ft open boat, the 'Glencoe', mainly to facilitate the transport of goods to their family shops which supplied provisions to the workforce at the head of Loch Leven. There was the facility to ferry a few passengers as well as goods. A regular service was set up in the autumn of 1905 with the addition of the 'Cona' to the fleet. This 35ft boat had capacity for 26 passengers and improved daily travel for employees. Facilities were further advanced with the purchase of the 'Dolphin' in 1907, and its licence for 34 passengers. The boat owners next formed a shipping company in 1908, the Loch Leven Shipping Co., to purchase a larger vessel to meet growing travel demand on the loch route, eventually procuring a Clyde ferry boat with the capacity for carrying 330 passengers. This boat was renamed the 'Loch Leven Queen.' It provided a regular daily service. But in 1911 John Grant gave up the service completely, undercut by competition from David MacBrayne Ltd., who went on to enjoy a monopoly until 1922 when the opening of the new south Loch Leven road to Kinlochleven village put an end to the need for sea route travel. This road, which had been constructed by German prisoners of war held in captivity at a camp near the Blackwater Dam, was much valued as it vastly improved access to Kinlochleven and its factory. The improvements next carried out on the rutted track that linked Onich and Kinlochleven, on the north side of Loch Leven, enabled round-the-loch access to Kinlochleven and so created a much less isolated 'City in the Hills.' All these developments brought better facilities to communities on and around Loch Leven. Better access, transport and job creation went hand in hand, much as Dr Grant had often predicted.

While the new industry in Kinlochleven strode to full production and matured as a workplace, many workers from Ballachulish turned their back on the older Argyllshire industry of quarrying to embrace factory work. In doing so they were seeing the benefit to themselves and their families in having regular, steady, well-paid employment. Work and welfare, as ever, were at the heart of the matter.

Over the years, Dr Grant remained loyal to the old slate quarrying industry of Argyllshire and his support to those employed in the Ballachulish quarries never faltered, even if he harboured doubts about those who filled the company's boardroom. In all fairness to him, he had cast the legal dispute with them from his mind and he remained positive and even-handed. His essay on the slate quarries of Ballachulish, composed in 1922, and which he entitled 'An Old Argyllshire Industry,' is a classic composition from the pen of Dr Grant. The article is included (p. 72) to exhibit Grant's style and his own line of thinking on industrial matters.

In terms of industry, work and welfare it could be supposed that, in the years from 1900 until the onset of the First World War, fortunes had flowed to a significant extent in Dr Grant's personal favour: he achieved his appointment as medical officer from a crowded field of talent; he was to regain his post after a legal battle; he nursed Kinlochleven to its triumph; he secured transport and freight improvements for North Lorn; he pressed for medical welfare and health service reforms through the Dewar Committee and saw the High-lands and Islands Medical Scheme delivered from 1913; and went on to fashion the National Health Service, whose keel was laid in his lifetime, though not launched till three years after he died in 1945. Sufficient achievement, one would suppose, to satisfy anyone's ambition. But not Lachlan Grant's.

Scarcely had one war ended, and before another one broke out, when Dr Grant was back in his stride. He entered a phase when he firmly believed the Government's neglect of the Highlands had to be faced and action had to be taken in order to 'save' the whole region.

The numerous organisations he set up were intended simply to take the fight for improvement directly to the door of government. Taking them in chronological order, the Crofters' and Cottars' Association was formed to better the lot of families making a livelihood from the land; the Sea League was formed to right the wrongs visited on the inshore fisherman and their families on the west coast and the islands by marauding and ruthless trawler fleets from the east coast; and the New Deal was a bid for a diversity of jobs, for new industries and for the modernisation of some old, embedded industries. To back up these engines, the Highland Development League was launched. It was geared to recruit the widest support from the Highlands and Islands, to articulate with one voice the stated aims drawn up in the New Deal Plan and to link with the Sea League and the Crofters and Cottars in a concerted effort to challenge the Government. It was incredible for Dr Grant, his colleagues and supporters, to observe just how indifferent governments were and how hopelessly ineffective Members of Parliament were found to be. Despite the many setbacks suffered, years and years of campaigning continued unabated, especially in the period between 1930 and 1939, while the Second World War intervened to strangle plans prepared and choke off progress. Nevertheless, there were optimists around, in good number, who envisaged better times ahead in the post-war era, and they held out. Improvements did take place, jobs did arise, and in the Highlands especially, revival came about, mainly on the basis of development plans for hydroelectric generation: a bright new industry, headed and ably led by Mr Tom Johnston, a former Secretary of State for Scotland, and a personal friend of Dr Lachlan Grant. The real impact of that industry was not felt until the War was past. Lachlan Grant understood its potential. He witnessed its birth, but he himself did not live to see it flourish so vigorously. In the end one could claim there was a 'City in the Hills,' and the light shone brightly in his beloved Highlands.

'SUIL AIR AIS...' (A Backward Glance)

It is little wonder that Dr Grant was so supportive of new industries like aluminium smelting in Kinlochleven. A look at the growing statistics would certainly have warmed him to the whole idea and put a song in his heart. For before him, he witnessed a remote rural hamlet of two farms with few employees, if any, in 1900 converted to the site of a major new industry, with supporting services, in full production by 1910. What was even more gratifying was the growth in the settled population at Kinlochleven from around 1911, by which time all the construction workers had left the site. According to the census returns for subsequent years, the Kinlochleven population was recorded as follows:

Year	Population
1911	1,189
1921	1,441
1931	1,610
1939	1,860

This was remarkable evidence to back Dr Grant's ongoing call for more industry in the Highlands. When one examines it, the fact remains; a lonely, empty glen of few people came to support over 1,000 men and women in the space of ten years, with that number rising to almost 2,000 before the Second World War. It was gratifying. But details of the employment which sustained this larger population would have mattered even more to Dr Grant. Census returns and the employment figures provided by the British Aluminium Company during and immediately after the First World War (1914-1919) recorded such data faithfully:

Year	Employees	
1914	644	(First World War began)
1915	600	
1916	600	
1917	584	
1918	730	
1919	640	(First World War ended)
1919	709	(post-War)
1920	589	
1920	810	
1920	752	

20 Blackwater Dam Construction

21 Construction of Water Pipes from Blackwater Dam to
Kinlochleven Power Station

There at a glance, one sees employment held up during the War and once hostilities ended there was a surge in demand for the metal; production increased to match and employment rose appreciably. The Kinlochleven area seemed to have been shielded from the recession which prevailed in many other parts of the nation. Yes, Dr Lachlan Grant could be satisfied on a number of counts. As he had overall medical responsibility for the residents of Kinlochleven, and all workers at the factory, no one was better placed to witness these matters at first hand.

'AN OLD ARGYLLSHIRE INDUSTRY'

In October 1922 Dr Grant wrote an article on Ballachulish and its slate quarries, which is an interesting account of a subject about which he had first-hand knowledge and much experience. The text of this particular essay is worth reproducing verbatim:

'Ballachulish, which signifies 'the town on the narrows', is a landmark of the Western Highlands, with an interesting history and curious traditions. Situated on the Argyllshire side of Loch Leven, an arm of Loch Linnhe, within a mile of Glencoe, it presents a striking picture as seen from the steamer or from the opposite side of the loch. The mountain rock-faces, deeply gashed and scarred in the quest for the famous roofing slate, with long rows of neat, whitewashed cottages in the foreground, attract attention. The rounded, towering Pap of Glencoe, a little way to the north, stands out as a silent sentinel pointing the way to the historic glen and the surrounding panorama of mountains add impressiveness to the scene.

While history and romance naturally direct your footsteps to the traditional site of the massacre, and up the wild and lonely glen, modern and industrial interests suggest a halt at the village of Ballachulish. It might well be named the 'village of slates', for its dwelling, dykes and roadways, gravestones and memorials, and the immense bings of shale all bear witness to the main occupation of the inhabitants. In the process of quarrying, the great, dark, frowning masses of rock debris have grown up as necessary evils and although they do not appeal to the eye of the artist, they are monuments of human efforts and not unregarded with pride by the descendents of many generations of quarrymen. Some authorities think that these excrescences may yet be utilised in some profitable way, for modern science, in its ubiquitous probing and researches, is discovering practical uses for many hitherto rejected by-products of industry.

It is not quite clear when slates first began to be quarried in Ballachulish. According to local tradition, the quarries were worked as far back as the days before the historic massacre of the MacDonalds, or over two hundred years ago, and authentic history goes back over a century. During that period there has been an immense output of the well-known blue roofing slates, yet experts assert that the supply still waiting to be worked is sufficient to last for many generations. Ballachulish slates are of the highest grade, with a special reputation for colour and durability, and until recent times the demand was equal to the supply, in spite of their cost being at times somewhat above those from Wales and elsewhere. While Welsh states are suitable for certain classes of buildings, the indigenous slates of Argyll, by reason of their hardness and superior colour, retaining and weathering qualities, are better suited for our northern climate, and the powerful disintegrating atmosphere of Glasgow, Edinburgh, Dundee, etc.

At the present time, the quarries are almost at a standstill. War conditions and the slump in the building trade have had an adverse effect on their prosperity. In 1918 negotiations were set afoot to reconstruct the quarries under Government auspices, and by the intervention of Sir William Sutherland M.P., a scheme was formed which received the approval of the Treasury. It was arranged that the 'Buildings Materials Supply Department' should take a lease of the quarries for ten years and work them as a national concern. But just as everything was thought ready to start on new lines and with up-to-date plant and machinery, some legal hitch occurred, and the scheme was held up and finally abandoned.

When the War ended, local efforts were made to restart the quarries, but such met with only partial success. In former times as many as 500 quarrymen were employed full time, while recently less than one-fifth of that number have been working, and with intervals of short time and stoppages. In consequence, many quarrymen, including a number of ex-service men, have had to look elsewhere for work. There has been want and distress in the district of late owing to the recent – let us hope temporary – cessation of work at the quarries.

The fine blue slate is there and the experienced quarrymen are on the spot, or still within call. The transit facilities by water, rail and road are excellent. Houses, schools, churches, water supply and other amenities are already existing. It only requires the intelligent co-operation of the workmen, the capitalist and the landowner, combined with modern go-ahead business methods to thoroughly revive this old Highland industry, and give it a further long lease of life and prosperity.

Lachlan Grant 1922'

The discourse is vintage Grant. It is well laid out, there is utmost respect for all parties involved, nothing said must prejudice employment, problems are not insolvable, there has to be an avenue of hope, the best minds must step forward, and the Government needs to be hooked. Dr Grant's style was to be pragmatic, never dogmatic. His ability to communicate with all classes of people was his great strength, and this he could do orally, in well-chosen words, or prose that was fluent, lucid, and learned.

While the slate industry had a rather chequered history, and its fortunes ebbed and flowed, trading feverishly thorough the many market ups and downs, there is no denying that the product itself was highly regarded and eagerly sought after throughout the Kingdom, in Europe, and even in America. Ballachulish slate was, and is, second to none: a by-word in quality roof cladding. It pretty well provided the entire roofing slate for the native cities of Edinburgh, Glasgow and Dundee. Undoubtedly, the quarries had a staunch supporter and passionate advocate in Dr Grant, as his article demonstrates, and he was forever the optimist in such matters. One way or another, Ballachulish quarries remained in operation up to, and past, the date of Dr Grant's death in 1945, but not much longer. They closed permanently in 1955.

With due regard and respect for the reputation of the slate quarried at Ballachulish, one has to accept there were drawbacks. For every hundred tons of slate cut from the quarry face, only twenty-five tons of useable dressed slate was produced for shipping out. There was thus a wastage rate of 75% and environmental problems created by the shale were distressing. In today's climate of opinion, and eco-friendliness, this would simply be unacceptable. Also, care had to be taken in the selection of slate itself, as the presence of iron pyrite in the rock could be detrimental. With weathering, the pyrite crystals rusted and left the affected slates pitted and holed. Quality control remains a must at all times.

At a personal level, Dr Grant enjoyed temporary employment in the quarry manager's office on leaving school. Dr Campbell of Craigrannoch held the lease at the time from the then landowner, Lady Elizabeth Beresford and the trustees of the late Sir George Beresford. During that period the quarries were reported as being 'worked with great vigour.' Employment level was recorded at 600 men, all trades included, and the quarrymen's earnings were quoted as being 20/- to 40/- per week. It was a time of some contentment and relative prosperity. When Dr Grant next played a role within the organisation it was as unanimously appointed medical officer to the quarrymen, their families, and the district generally. This role he took up in August 1900 and no one could possibly have foreseen or foretold the turmoil ahead of them. The quarry lease had been in the hands of a private limited company since 1895, and under the chairmanship of one almighty unpopular figure, Col. Edward D. Malcolm of Poltalloch. He appointed Mr Archibald MacColl, a local figure, as works manager at the quarries. Work there continued, albeit in an increasingly restless setting. Without any warning or notice, the popular doctor was suddenly dismissed by the company, and forbidden to practise within the district. In such fashion, the first lockout took place at the quarries. Work closed down completely, and a bitter dispute raged on for 18 months. While this historic episode is covered in detail elsewhere in the book, the silver lining had to be that resolution did take place, ultimately; the quarrymen returned to their stations and Dr Grant was fully reinstated in this former post, without restriction. There was even more satisfaction in the fact that he went on to provide professional medical service until his death in 1945. Ironic it may seem, but the quarries were to operate for a further ten years after the natural demise of its medical officer, when in 1955 work finally closed down. Thus, an 'Old Argyllshire Industry' had also had its day.

8

The Family

Lachlan Grant was fortunate to grow up in a stable, moral and loving family who, at every turn, demonstrated social responsibility and remained mindful of the needs of fellow beings. His ancestors, in their own capacity, had proved their worth in their chosen spheres of life, and made success of it. Such background and stability did serve Lachlan and his siblings well throughout their lives. They did not have far to go in search of role models; the evidence is that they did not need to travel beyond the family ranks.

While his own family life was so sound, it is quite remarkable that Lachlan did not experience married life until his later years. He remained a bachelor right up to his 44th year. His bachelor accommodation was to be wherever duties took him: Edinburgh, Oban, the Isle of Skye, and Ballachulish itself. His move 'home' in 1900 certainly took him back near the bosom of the family, but he rented premises of his own at Ardarroch in West Laroch, and later at Laroch House in Loanfern; both addresses were within the village and within easy walking distance of the parental home at Barr's Store or the Cottage at Glencoe. In that regard, he likely had the benefit of the female family members 'doing' for him and supporting him fully in the domestic sense as it seems they were wont to do for the other male members of the family who were fully occupied with running the family business at Ballachulish and Kinlochleven. Family members were all remarkably supportive of one another and operated from day to day as a team, without quibble.

Romance did eventually blossom but it was not until 1915 that he took as his bride the young and talented local lady, Catherine (Katie) Clark. On the day of their wedding, 30 March 1915, Katie was only in her nineteenth year. The marriage took place in Edinburgh and the reception was held in the North British Hotel, nowadays known as 'the Balmoral.' Their marriage banns, as posted in advance, were read in the United Free Church at home. Attendants were: bridesmaid, Miss Violet McIntosh; best man, Dr William Murdie and as witness, Mr James Meldrum. Dr Murdie, a native of Stronchrubie in Assynt, Sutherlandshire, was one of Dr Grant's earliest medical assistants in Kinlochleven and they remained firm friends throughout life. At the time of marriage Katie Clark was working in Edinburgh as a teacher of domestic science at the Edinburgh College of Domestic Science at 5 Atholl Crescent – the prestigious city college that schooled many generations of young women in culinary and home-making skills. It was a training that served her well as she settled into her new way of life, the young wife of a very busy medical practitioner, back in their home village in Argyll. Their first marital home was in rented accommodation at Laroch House, Loanfern. In 1916 their first child, Sheena, was born, followed by their second daughter, Marie, in 1919. The year 1922 saw the birth at Laroch House of Eleanora Isabella Stewart Grant, their third daughter and the last child born to the family. All three children grew up initially with their parents at Laroch House and received their early education from a private governess, Miss Saunders. Marie and Eleanora later enrolled at Ballachulish Public School, on 12 March 1929, at the respective ages of 10 and 7 years. Eleanora was to re-register on 19 August 1930, and remained at school there until transferring to Oban High School in August 1934, at the age of 12 years. Sheena, on the other hand, transferred from the care of the governess to St George's School for Girls in Edinburgh, where she paved the way for her younger sister Marie to join her later on. The two eldest girls progressed through their private school most successfully and on to college and university training. Eleanora also achieved highly at Oban High School and took many class prizes as she progressed through the school.

A major change in all their lives came about when Dr and Mrs Grant commissioned building work on their new house at West Laroch in 1928. Dr Grant called on the services of the architectural firm, Kerr & Watson, from Johnstone, (his old home town) to draw up plans to his specification for a commodious house with an ample practice surgery suite attached. Craigleven was thus conceived and commissioned, and completed by the end of 1929. From rented accommodation at Laroch House the family moved, in 1929, to their freshly finished home, and were justly proud in doing so. At that significant moment in time, the girls were respectively 13, 10, and 7 years of age.

A priority for Dr Grant, on moving premises, was the setting up of a professionally equipped laboratory. He was most passionate about the early investigation, detection, and treatment of diseases and was fully convinced it was the best way to better outcomes for patients. As a matter of interest, his professional address was given not as, 'the Surgery, Ballachulish,' or some such typical address, but was publicised without fail as: 'The Bacteriological Laboratories, Ballachulish, Argyll'.

He went further and proudly proclaimed himself also to be, by appointment, 'The Bacteriologist, District Committees, Argyll County Council, and Medical Officer, Fever Hospital, Lorn.'

Mrs Grant wasted no time in putting her home-making skill to use. Craigleven soon came to be a hive of activity, yet a haven of peace and happiness. There was a warm welcome for visitors and there were many of them from near and far. Hospitality in the household became legendary and Katie Grant's talents for baking, cooking, and serving up delicious and nutritious meals were renowned among all friends and acquaintances. More attractive still was her constant habit of exercising her vocal chords, singing her sweet Gaelic songs (she was a mezzo-soprano of Mod Gold Medal standard) while busying herself around the home. Amazingly, older patients in the practice in my time fondly recalled the music and kitchen aromas that percolated through from the house to the surgery as they sat in a row waiting to consult the doctor. The same flavour is given by Mr Duncan Clark, a nephew of Katie Grant who, as a young boy, spent periods of his life living with his aunt while his mother struggled with months of illness in hospital in the far north east of Scotland. He not only returned his aunt's love; he noted how lovely a person she was and how patient and organised she was in every single thing she did. That by itself is a fine and moving testimony, at first hand, from a sensitive young boy.

The three girls related well to their parents and family holidays and entertainment were always attended to. Social events were embraced in some style; celebrations of 21st birthdays, for example, were enthusiastically observed.

Within the family, care was taken to ensure a balanced life was led and, beyond work, leisure activities were encouraged. Dr Grant himself was a keen golfer who regularly played on the local golf course and who presided over the club's affairs. He likewise encouraged the 'good old game of shinty' among all the young boys and the healthier adult males and, there again, he was the Chieftain of the Ballachulish Camanachd Club as well as a generous supporter. His less physical pursuits included playing the piano, by ear it seems, and lending musical accompaniment to Mrs Grant's solo singing, on public platforms as well as in private settings. Being an expert on eyes, the principles of light waves and photography were only too well understood by him and camera work was a big hobby of his, enabling him to keep a fine album as well as a film record of all family activities over the years. Books, reading and writing were always a major part of his life and he loved to keep abreast of new developments in various fields, many unconnected with medicine. When they moved to Craigleven, newly-built tennis courts were readily to hand for the girls, their school friends and visitors to enjoy to the maximum. The prevailing attitude within and outwith the home was undoubtedly 'mens sana in corpore sano.' Being the classicist he was, Dr Grant needed no reminding of such ancient values and virtues.

University success was another source of pleasure, giving rise to celebra-

22 The family relax by the seaside in North Lorn
From left: Eleanora, Marie, Sheena, Katie, Dr Lachlan

tions. The local press, especially *The Oban Times*, was meticulous in covering news items of the kind and sharing them with its readership in general. For example, in the issue of 31 July 1941:

'University success. Among those capped at the recent graduation ceremony in Edinburgh University we are pleased to note the name of Dr Marie Paton Shedden Grant, who passed MB ChB degrees. Dr Grant is the 2nd eldest daughter of Dr Lachlan Grant J.P., Ballachulish.'

Following her graduation in Edinburgh, Dr Marie then spent a few months assisting her father in his practice. Again her progress was watched and reported on in local newspapers:

'10th October 1942. Dr Marie P.S. Grant MB ChB has now left the area to take up the post of House Physician of the Simpson Memorial

Wards at the Royal Infirmary Edinburgh, in the charge of Prof. Robert Johnstone.'

Family engagements are always a thrill and the Grant household had such an experience in 1943 when daughter Sheena made her intentions known. In *The Scotsman* on 18 September 1943, the formal announcement was made:

'Mr R.A. Roddan – Miss S. Grant
The engagement is announced between Robert Alexander Roddan BSc, AMIEE, AMICE, youngest son of the late Mr and Mrs John Roddan, Dumfries, and Sheena, eldest daughter of Dr Lachlan Grant MD, DPH, FRFPS, and Mrs Grant, Craigleven, Ballachulish, Argyll.'

Their wedding in April 1944 received national coverage and was a smart affair held at St Giles' Cathedral in Edinburgh and celebrated with 100 guests at the North British Hotel, the same venue as her parents had chosen for their big day. As was typical of the era, every detail merited a mention.

'Highland Wedding at St Giles' Cathedral.
Roddan – Grant
The wedding took place in the Moray Aisle of St Giles' Cathedral, Edinburgh of April 21st of Miss Sheena grant, daughter of Dr Lachlan Grant and Mrs Grant, Craigleven, Ballachulish. Dr Grant, who is well known in the Highlands Gaelic circles as chairman of the Highland Development League, gave away his daughter. The bridegroom, Mr Robert Alexander Roddan AIMEE., AMICE., is on the staff of British Aluminium Co. Ltd., and is the youngest son of Mr and Mrs John Roddan, Dumfries. The ceremony was conducted by the Very Rev. Charles Warr CVO, DD, Dean of the Thistle, assisted by the Rev. John MacKay MA, Ballachulish. The bridesmaids were Dr Marie Grant and Miss Eleanora Grant (sisters of the bride) and the best man was Mr Alan R. Wylie, Kinlochleven. The bridegroom's presents to the bride included a necklace of gold and pearls with matching brooch, and to the bridesmaids he presented brooches, one of turquoise and gold and the other coral and gold.'

The occasion was a big day, all the niceties were attended to, and no detail missing. Dr and Mrs Grant had once more performed proudly and with propriety, and had done honour to the newly-wed couple and all their guests.
Eleanora performed well academically at school, and effortlessly passed

through classes. She also shone at competition singing at all the local Gaelic Mods in Argyll and at the Annual National Mod itself. Having inherited her mother's gift and talent in music and singing, she demonstrated the fact with all the silverware and gold pendants she accumulated. Her decision to follow a career in the Royal Navy was unusual for a woman at that time but one she took enthusiastically and she was subsequently, during WW2, selected to serve on special wartime tasks at Bletchley Park – marking her keen intelligence. In later years she was engaged in the British nuclear industry as a public relations officer. She remained a spinster and retired contentedly in Edinburgh among a close circle of friends. She died in January 2002.

Dr Marie devoted her life to her profession. She had a particular interest in the welfare of women and women's health issues, and gave years of service to Fife Health Board. She read avidly, possessed a shrewd mind and had a beady eye for all the best investments. In her person and profession she mirrored much of her father. She too never married but, like Eleanora, she enjoyed many friendships beyond the family and retired to Edinburgh, where she ended her days in March 1994.

Sheena was the only member of the family to marry, and she and Robert kept home in various parts of Scotland, be it Inverness-shire, Falkirk, Edinburgh, or Stirlingshire. Their only daughter, Susan, remains the bearer and carrier of the great Grant genes. She is happily married to a fine man, Hector MacLennan, who spent his working life in the whisky marketing business, and whose hospitality knows no bounds at all. With Glasgow and Rogart connections, Hector is a scion of that MacLennan clan who have immersed themselves, variously in medicine, gynaecology, the law and politics. Sadly, of Hector and Susan's two sons, Niall died young playing sport, while resident in Arizona, USA. Happily though, Lorne remains with us and he and his delightful wife, Julia, have now ensured that the Grant line will survive, with the recent birth of a son, Finlay Hector Douglas.

Dr Lachlan Grant and his charming, talented wife Katie did all that they possibly could to improve the lot of others. They spared nothing for the future of other family members as well as their own children. The harvest was worth reaping, and all who know them have been enriched by the experience. Lachlan Grant attained the 'promised age': his track record unrivalled, he passed away peacefully at Craigleven, surrounded by his devoted family, in 1945. In the end, however, life could have dealt a much kinder hand to his dear wife for she herself died at Craigleven in 1947, only two years after her husband, while still a young lady. Those who knew her best knew she deserved a better lot.

A PERSONAL PROFILE

Early photographic albums in the family show that Lachlan Grant was a man of spare frame, lean and fit in appearance. Of average height, his dress and deportment complemented his overall physical looks and gave the impression of one who very much cared about being 'dressed for the part.' His dress code, as a doctor, was that of your typical consultant in a city hospital, and would have been identical to the style worn by the clinical chiefs in Edinburgh Royal Infirmary in Grant's day as medical student, undergraduate, and house doctor. The dark sober suit, or frocked coat with striped trousers, complete with dark waistcoat across which ran a gold link-chain, with fob, to pocket watch, was classic consultant attire. Accessories to be added were the bowler or silk top hat, white linen or cotton gloves, well-polished or patent laced black shoes, plus gaiters, spats or galoshes as determined by the weather. Shirts were white, with or without winged collar but always with a silk tie and jewelled tiepin. A stick, or cane, in hand seemed to add authority, or a touch of the military, to the wearer's bearing. As a Highland GP, such attire was completely at odds with the garb of Gaels generally and with that worn by country doctors in the Highlands particularly, who could easily be mistaken for gamekeepers! Their

23 'Self Drive'

cladding was commonly tweed (and wool) from head to toe; often plus-fours, a deer-stalker or tweed fishing-hat and footwear of brown brogues, of a robustness that suggested Clyde ship-building! A country doctor's leisure interests were also taken for granted: fishing, shooting and hunting. In all respects Grant differed so much; he cut an Edwardian figure, eschewed field-sports, loved the golf links, relished photography and cultivated cerebral interests like reading, writing and politics. With the exception of the 'good old game of shinty,' or Camanachd, to which he was devoted, it could be said Dr Grant was atypical of his professional country peers. It is fascinating to note that, though he was a regular at Gaeldom's ceilidhs and concerts, Mods and meetings, he never wore Highland dress or sported the kilt at any time. What his great friend, his 'caraid,' the constantly kilted Johnnie Bannerman, had to say about the matter is not placed on record. Bannerman wore his own MacDonald tartan proudly.

Unlike his fellow rural practitioners, Dr Grant was not one afflicted by the West Highland weakness, for he partook little by way of alcohol and only on such social occasions as befitted. In such settings he was a model of good behaviour and responsibility. It is true that his family background, on both the Grant and Paton sides, was strongly opposed to imbibing alcohol, and strongly linked to the Temperance movement, as well as adherent to the Free and United Free Churches. One can safely assume that Dr Grant would be moderate, and not given to extremes, when it came to social drinking. One habit of social interest is that he was a cigarette smoker throughout his early professional career. It seems that in later life he only succumbed, in the words of the family, to 'the odd one for the midges!'

In summary, he was a professional man whose good manners and wise discretion made him, in everyone's view, 'a safe pair of hands,' to be taken at his word and trusted. As a communicator, he was comfortable with people drawn from all walks of life and practised no prejudice. His academic record and cerebral might were widely known and recognised, but he never flaunted these attributes. Apart from his own family, he likely rated his friends and many friendships his treasure trove, and experience throughout his life had riveted him to the value and virtue of loyalty. How fitting that such an attribute was encapsulated so succinctly in the Grant clan motto: 'Stand Fast!'

THE CLARK FAMILY, BALLACHULISH

The Clark family, into which Dr Grant married in 1915, was a deeply rooted Highland family, steeped in Gaelic language and culture. John Clark's family were Ballachulish people down the generations. His wife, Mary Ferguson, was a native of Shawbost, Isle of Lewis, and thus a Hebridean by descent. John

Clark, like his fore-fathers, spent all his working his life as a quarrier at the local slate quarries in Ballachulish.

John Clark and Mary Ferguson were married in Glasgow on 23 April 1881 and following marriage made their family home back in Ballachulish, at 10 West Laroch. It was there they reared and brought up their family of ten: seven sons and three daughters. As parents they were a hard-working and honest couple, who provided as best they could for their children and saw to their upbringing and education in a most dutiful manner. It is a credit to both parents that their children all grew up and matured to be outstanding individuals, who rose to be successful in later life. The Clark family comprised:

Angus Clark, b. 1881, d. 1945 (64), at Stirling
Duncan, b. 1883, d. 1912 (29), at Ballachulish
Donald, b. 1885, d. 1970 (85), at Inverkeithing
James, b. 1887, d. 1935 (48), at Stirling
John, b. 1890, d. 1956 (66), at Stirling (f. to Dr Iain)
Neil, b. 1891, d. 1891, at Ballachulish
Margaret, b. 1891, d. 1971 (80), at Ballachulish
Annie, b. 1893, d. 1977 (84), at Glencoe
Dugald, b. 1895, d. 1924 (29), at Ballachulish
Catherine, b. 1896, d. 1947 (51), at Ballachulish

John Clark died in 1921, aged 67 years, and his wife Mary passed away in 1936, aged 80 years. They lived all their days at Ballachulish. The children were brought up in the village and received their schooling at Ballachulish Public School. Of them all it was to be the eldest and the youngest members who were to play a major and central role in Lachlan Grant's life: Angus and Catherine (Katie) Clark.

Though Angus was ten years younger than Lachlan, it is well to remember they both grew up in the same village and, for a time, attended the same local school. The gap in age did, however, highlight their separate paths as well. For example when Lachlan matriculated in medicine in 1889, Angus Clark was still an eight-year old schoolboy back home. Likewise, at the time when Grant graduated as a doctor (1894), the young lad, Angus, was still at school. It is likely, therefore, that there was little association between the two of them until 1900, when Dr Grant returned to Ballachulish, on taking up his post there. At that stage Dr Grant was 29 years of age and Angus Clark was, as a 19 year old, employed in the slate quarries. Initially he was engaged as a quarrier, but soon gained a role in the manager's office as a cashier and bookkeeper, later stepping into the role of the elected leader of the quarrymen's trade union. It appears

24 Catherine Grant (née Clark),
c. 1915

likely that it was at this time, around August 1900, that the two men 'bonded.' They did so especially through Angus Clark's own important involvement in trade unionism and politics. What is not in doubt is how exceptionally deep and mutually respectful the friendship was destined to be: unshakeable to the end. By a strange coincidence, given the age difference, they were to depart this life in the same year: Dr Grant on 31 May and Angus Clark on 26 September 1945.

In family terms, the Grant/Clark relationship was destined to extend well beyond Angus Clark, when, in 1915, Lachlan Grant married Angus's sister Katie, the youngest of the Clarks, becoming brother-in-law to his best friend, Angus. With the families united in marriage, roles changed but bonds strengthened. Dr Grant's marriage to Katie did not pass without comment; he had been a 'confirmed' bachelor until he entered his forty-fourth year, and his bride was a young lady just turned nineteen. Unsurprisingly, there was an element of doubt as to the prospects for such a marriage among some members of their respective families, while others were generous in their support. But all such doubt was misplaced: the marriage was one of mutual love, respect and support. The fact was that both lives were enriched, the one as much as the other. From the first day of marriage Katie and Lachlan Grant set up a home that was forever to be an oasis of happiness. Union of the families undoubtedly deepened the friendships that had earlier existed and set the seal of success on the generations that were to follow. Both Katie and her brother Angus carved out interesting lives of their own and demonstrated abilities and talents that were truly impressive. In that respect, by way of explanation and emphasis, one needs to outline the personal profile and qualities of each of them, as they both played so central a role in the life and times of Dr Lachlan Grant.

Firstly, Mrs Grant deserves to take the stage for that is one thing she did in her life, with poise and confidence. A feature of her whole life was the degree to which she could multi-task and perform so many roles both in private and in the public arena. She was not one to neglect her husband and her family, her home or her community, or the needs of others. She and her husband spared not in their support of charities and culture, especially the Gaelic culture and the beloved National Mods and Highland Societies. A flavour of her devotion to such causes is conveyed in the following account of her good works.

CATHERINE GRANT – HIGHLIGHTS OF A SINGING CAREER

Katie Grant was blessed with a very fine singing voice (mezzo soprano) and sang at many functions throughout her life: publicly, privately, socially at fundraising events and competitively at local and national annual Gaelic Mods. She gained many gold medals for solo singing, especially the Oran Mor entries, but the Mod Gold Medal itself eluded her; she was runner-up on frequent occasions and at the 35th Annual National Mod in Dingwall in 1931 she tied with

Miss Helen T MacMillan for the prize. On reviewing the marks attained by both competitors the adjudicators, on balance, awarded the Gold Medal for that year to Helen T MacMillan, who went to a glorious career, singing Gaelic at home and abroad. To tie with Helen T MacMillan was no mean feat in itself. Was she not one of three daughters of Mr Angus MacMillan, a native of Islay and a schoolmaster at Dervaig, Isle of Mull, who all became Mod gold medallists? For the record, Annie MacMillan won the Fort William Mod in 1922, Helen T won the Dingwall Mod in 1931, and Mae Margaret the 1947 Perth Mod; an astounding family record of solo singing success.

25 Helen T MacMillan

Mrs Grant was a fluent native Gaelic speaker and, of course, a native of Ballachulish as well. So it is interesting to browse over a few of those public appearances and especially her Mod performances. It may be added that daughter Eleanora, like her mother, was a gifted singer too, and won numerous prizes at the local Junior Mods held in Argyll, as well as in the junior section of National Mods.

1931   35th Annual National Mod in Dingwall:
Senior section – Female, Comunn Gaidhealtachd member
1st: Mrs Catherine Grant
(Oran Mor – An Domhnallach Deas)

Ladies Gold Medal 1931:
1st: Miss Helen T MacMillan
2nd: Mrs Catherine Grant

Solo Singing – Competition 47 – Ladies
1st: Mrs Catherine Grant

Mod success in 1931 led to a spate of invitations to sing at many distinguished
Highland gatherings and concerts held by Highland 'expats' in cities such as
Glasgow and Edinburgh. Among these was, typically, a full billing at the Clan
Cameron Concert at the Berkeley Halls in Glasgow – a grand social affair.

1932   36th Annual National Mod in Fort William
(This Mod was attended by J. Ramsay MacDonald)
Ladies Gold Medal 1932
2nd: Mrs Catherine Grant

26 Dr and Mrs Grant take leave of J Ramsay MacDonald, 1932

1933   37th Annual National Mod in Glasgow
While Mrs Grant claimed her share of the prizes it was daughter Eleanora who, with her success in the Junior Mod competitions, made the headlines. The Glasgow Evening News on 26th September 1933 was to proclaim: 'Eleanora Grant, the daughter of Dr & Mrs Lachlan Grant, of Ballachulish, a young prize-winner at the National Mod in Glasgow today.'

1934   38th Annual National Mod in Oban
Back on home territory, and the birth-place of the Mod itself, the competing and the success continued to excite Mod followers.
    1st: Mrs Catherine Grant – Ladies Oran Mor

1935   39th Annual Mod in Edinburgh
    Ladies Gold Medal 1935
    2nd: Mrs Catherine Grant

Annually, the National Mod generated huge interest among the Gaels, and led to ceilidhs being held to bring performers to a still wider audience around the country. On 28 April 1930 a fund-raising organ recital at St Columba's Church in Glasgow featured:

    Soloist: Mrs Catherine Grant, Ballachulish
    Organist: Mr G.M. Loynd

Less sedate maybe, and infinitely more vibrant was the 1933 Caledonian Medical Society Dinner in London, where Mrs Grant entertained with a selection of Gaelic songs and Dr George MacKinnon, a GP and native of South Uist, gave a robust and rousing recital on the Highland pipes. Fund-raising events were occurring regularly over the autumn and winter season, and ranged from the City Halls in Glasgow and Edinburgh, the Town Hall of Inverness to, nearer home, the much loved Argyllshire Gathering Halls in Oban.
    Many local and national charities and 'good causes,' as well as the Gaelic movement, benefited greatly from monies thus raised, and Catherine Grant, for one, gave generously and unstintingly of her time and talent to make that happen.

ANGUS CLARK – PROFILE OF DR GRANT'S TRUSTY FRIEND
Angus Clark was Katie Grant's eldest brother and Dr Grant's brother-in-law, as noted. But he was more than that: he was a man of might, whom many

would say was Dr Grant's 'rock' in times of trouble and his backbone in battles. One only has to study the role he played in the quarries dispute to realise that fact. He may have left the local school at the age of fourteen and gone straight to work as a quarrier but he was mentally quick enough to grasp things and to cope with steep learning curves though he was largely self-educated. From 1900 it seemed he ran the management and the workforce at the Ballachulish slate quarries. Moreover, his reputation as a 'straight sort of guy' was recognised by all parties.

When trouble did, unexpectedly, break out at the quarries it was Clark who led the men; it was Clark who crystallised the issues at stake; it was Clark who masterminded the campaigns and the fund-raising. Admittedly, Dr Grant did defend himself well, and carried himself with great dignity throughout. And the quarrymen's committee was composed of sane, sensible men, who were acute, astute and able. So Dr Grant was seen as being well served and supported in his personal fight for justice.

Throughout the years of the dispute, the strike and the legal battles, Angus Clark was to the fore. He was a clever man who was fluent in both Gaelic and English and, what was more, he was a gifted orator; so gifted in fact that his working colleagues at the quarries nicknamed him 'Balfour'! Clark was a passionate man who felt strongly about political matters, social issues, working conditions, job creation, revitalising the Highlands, supporting the Gaelic language and culture, and striving for the Scottish nation again. In early days he was unquestionably socialist in his political leanings, but he soon became dissatisfied and disillusioned with the lethargy, inertia, and inability of all southern-based governments. To him, Westminster rule was hopeless where action was required. So it was no surprise that Angus Clark became an ardent Scottish patriot who went on, with others, to form the National Party of Scotland, later the Scottish National Party. He remained based in Ballachulish until 1906 when he moved to London. There he was employed as a cashier and later head cashier in the East India Docks by the British India Steam Navigation Company Ltd., who amalgamated with P&O in 1914. Over the next 30 years, to 1936, he progressed to management within the company while at the same time developing his own business interests in quarrying, mining and importing stone for road-building works. He prospered well in these endeavours and gathered some wealth.

In London he continued with his political pursuits and his cultural interest in Gaelic extended to his election as the President of the Gaelic Society of London – an august body formed in 1777 for the purpose of promoting the welfare of the Highlands in the aftermath of Culloden. It claims to be the oldest Gaelic Society in the world. As far as Angus Clark was concerned, it gave him the perfect perch and platform, with authority to speak out against all the iniquities being perpetrated against the Highlanders, their culture and language. He was also a founding member of the Highland Club of London and its first elected president. All he did through these organisations and in the Highland Development League, he did in the name of his country and for the good of his fellow Scots and Highlanders. He made his return to Scotland in 1936 to advance political aims and to stimulate employment in quarrying and the national supply of stone. In ventures of this kind, he invested much of his personal wealth: in Brecklet slate quarries in 1936, in the white quartzite quarry at Onich in 1937, and at a later date, in the limestone quarry at Torlundy. After Angus Clark's death in 1945 the Torlundy quarry was bought over by Mr J W Hobbs of the Great Glen Cattle Ranch, Inverlochy Castle, and McNabb's distillery fame.

All in all, Angus Clark was a man of action and a man of his word. He returned to his roots in Ballachulish where he created work and welfare among his own people. In many respects he and Dr Grant were two of a kind: dynamic, progressive, articulate and fearless. They saw no obstacle in the way that could not be cleared, and they saw no ceiling to what could be achieved. From modest homes and common background, their achievements were truly impressive and arose from the talent they had inherited. Katie Clark, or Grant, could be just as proud of her own brother as she was of her diligent husband.

Obituary in *The Scotsman* in 1945

Mr Angus Clark, quarry master, Stirling, and late Assistant Controller of the stone trade in Scotland died yesterday at Causewayhead, Stirling, at the age of 64.

A native of Ballachulish, Mr Clark went to London as a young man, and was for 30 years with the British India Steam Navigation Company, for 20 of them being head cashier of the Royal Albert Dock, London. He was for a term president of the Gaelic Society of London, and was one of the originators and first president of the Highland Club of London. He returned to Scotland in 1936, and took an active part in the Scottish Nationalist movement. He was a prominent member of the Highland Development League. In 1938 Mr Clark took over the Stirling Quarry Company. On becoming Assistant Controller of the stone trade he lived for a time in Edinburgh.

He is survived by his wife and a son.

9

Friendships and Fellowships Forged

REV DUNCAN MACMURCHY

The Rev Duncan MacMurchy arrived in Ballachulish in 1878, two years before the Grant family moved north from Johnstone. MacMurchy was born in 1840 and would thus be 38 years old at the time he was inducted as the United Free Church minister at Brecklet. Lachlan Grant was a nine or ten-year old boy when he enrolled at Ballachulish Public School on 26 April 1880. It is not certain what part the church did play in Lachlan Grant's life, or which church the Grants as a family attended. Certainly, the family background was United Free Church and, likely, they adhered to that denomination. As to a personal contact through education, Duncan MacMurchy was for years the chairman of the school board of Ballachulish Public School, visited frequently and took a great interest in the education of all the local schoolchildren, and in each individually. However, his contact with Dr Lachlan Grant went a good deal beyond that, for he tutored Grant after he left the Public School in preparation for university entrance. MacMurchy was a very learned man, well read in Classics. He tutored young Lachlan in Latin and Greek. Coaching likely continued from the boy's fourteenth year until he was sent to Mr Boag's private college in Glasgow in 1889. Thereafter, personal contact and growing adult friendship with the minister would have been minimal until Grant returned to the village as the local doctor. From then their friendship certainly deepened and matured and in their professional capacity they worked in unity. The extent of the personal regard they had for one another was never more apparent than when the quarry dispute erupted: the Rev Duncan MacMurchy was one of Grant's most ardent supporters. Throughout the legal fight from 1903 to 1907, and the massive fund-raising effort, he never wavered in his support for the doctor. They shared a keen interest in the Ballachulish Public School and supported the headmaster and staff at all school functions, such as prize giving and Christmas parties. The close friendship continued until MacMurchy's death in 1921. Duncan MacMurchy died in harness, still in the ministry at the age of 81 years. He had served the local community well for 43 years. Dr Grant had every reason to be grateful to him, and he was.

MacMurchy must have been an exceptional individual for in 1891, 12 years on from his induction, it is recorded in '*The History of St Munda, Glencoe,*' that a local ecumenical grouping, backed by a large local deputation, gathered at the Free Church manse to present to him 'in the name of the people of Ballachulish' a valuable mantel clock and a purse containing 102 sovereigns. His sister, Miss MacMurchy, was presented with a silver tea set. The deputation comprised Church of Scotland, Episcopalian, Roman Catholic and Free Church adherents; the inscription on the clock read: 'Presented by the people of Ballachulish and other friends as a token of goodwill, personal regard, and in recognition of his varied public service as pastor and friend.' A remarkable demonstration of esteem.

DR JAMES B. SIMPSON C.B.E.

James Bertie Simpson belonged to Golspie and was a graduate of Edinburgh University, gaining an MB, CM in 1887. He proceeded to MD in 1892 after a period of study at Leipzig and Vienna. In 1889 he was appointed medical officer to the Ballachulish Slate Quarries Company and GP to Ballachulish and Glencoe district and served there until 1892, when he settled back in Golspie. Dr Simpson was of course GP to the Grant family during those years in 'the Glen' and formed a friendship with Lachlan Grant, then aged between 18 years (a medical student) and 23 years (a medical graduate). Their friendship endured and on Dr Grant's death in 1945, it was J. B. Simpson who provided his obituary for the *BMJ*, published in the issue 16 June 1945.

27 Dr James Bertie Simpson

Dr Simpson greatly advanced his own career and reputation over a long and successful life. He was elected FRCPEd in 1925 and was appointed a deputy lieutenant for the county of Sutherland. He was awarded the OBE in 1920 and was made CBE in 1942. He served with rare distinction many medical committees at county and national level and, as a keen BMA man, he well represented his colleagues who completely trusted him. Moreover, he successfully ran a large medical practice and his energy and perfection in all his activities was a source of amazement to all who knew him. It was only to be expected that he had become a household name in the northern counties and was referred to as 'Simpson of Golspie.' He also founded a medical dynasty: his son, Mr Soutar Simpson, became the consulting surgeon to the county of Sutherland and his grandson, Dr Michael M. Simpson, served the Golspie general medical practice for many years until his retirement.

Undoubtedly, despite the age difference, Dr Simpson and Dr Grant were of similar standing and reputation in their profession and among their native Highlanders. Dr Simpson died in Edinburgh in 1948 at the age of 85 years, outliving his younger friend by three years.

British Medical Journal, 4 December 1948
Obituary: J B Simpson, CBE, MD, FRCPEd.

Dr James Bertie Simpson, of Golspie, died on Nov. 16 in Edinburgh at the age of 85. Dr. Simpson was a student at Edinburgh University and graduated MB, CM in 1887, proceeding M.D. in 1892 after a period of study at Leipzig and Vienna. He was elected FRCPEd. in 1925, and was a deputy lieutenant for the county of Sutherland. He was awarded the OBE in 1920 and was made CBE in 1942. Dr. Simpson was an assistant in Ballachulish, Argyle, before settling in Golspie. He was chairman of the Caithness and Sutherland Division in 1922-3 and again in 1941. He had been a member of the Highlands and Islands Consultative Council and of the Insurance Acts Subcommittee for Scotland. He was an active member of the Scottish Committee from 1933-40 and again in 1945-6. He was also a representative at Annual Representative Meetings on several occasions.

Dr. D.W.D. MacLaren writes: With the passing of Dr. J.B. Simpson our profession in the north of Scotland mourns the loss of its most honoured and distinguished representative. 'Simpson of Golspie' was indeed a household word in all our northern counties. His devoted work over many years on behalf of his medical colleagues can never be forgotten. He was a keen and enthusiastic 'BMA man,' holding the highest of positions in his division and branch, and for years the trusted delegate to its national councils and committees in Edinburgh. His dynamic and colourful personality found scope in so many local and county activities that it is always a source of amazement how he found time for them all. In addition he ran a large and most successful general practice, and was medical superintendent of the county hospital at Golspie. He had the highest ideals and principles, and he was always a wise guide and friend to all who sought his advice. With his natural gifts of mind and heart he brought exceptional skill and competence to his professional work in Sutherland, that county which he served so well and which he loved so much. We shall always recall the energetic figure, the fresh complexion, the twinkling eye, the ready wit – caustic at times, but never vindictive – and the abounding humour, wise judgement, and shrewd Scottish common sense of this remarkable doctor, sportsman, and friend. To his son, Mr B Soutar Simpson, consulting surgeon to the county of Sutherland, who continues the family tradition, and to all those near and dear to him we offer heartfelt sympathy.

Dr. R. W. Craig writes: With a cultured mind and a capacity for shrewd judgement Dr J.B. Simpson combined a rich sense of humour and a strong appreciation of the finer things in life. Straight as a die, he could not tolerate humbug in any shape or form. His penetrating eye, despite its twinkle, could exert an influence which was frequently both chastening and astonishing. As a raconteur he was inimitable, and to spend an evening in Simpson's company was a most refreshing and delightful experience. To the British Medical Association he gave ungrudging and loyal service, but it was only natural that his chief interest should lie in the work of the Highlands and Islands subcommittee, of which he was chairman for many years. It was in large measure due to his influence that the Highlands and Islands Medical Service achieved its worldwide reputation. In the home of the crofter or the laird he was equally beloved and respected. He was a keen angler and an expert deerstalker. He kept himself fully abreast of the latest developments in medical science, and this is reflected in the fact that the late Sir John Fraser was glad on occasion to give his class of clinical surgery the opportunity of having a lecture from Dr. Simpson. A fine example of the best type of family doctor, his character and work will remain an inspiration to all who had the privilege of knowing him.

PROF. DOUGLAS ARGYLL ROBERTSON

Professor Douglas Moray Cooper Lamb Argyll Robertson enjoyed a medical career every bit as striking as his christened name. Known widely as Douglas Argyll Robertson, his is, to this day, a name and reputation known to every Scottish medical student for over a century. Robertson was a Scot and a distinguished graduate (1857) in medicine from the University of St Andrews. He pursued further study in Berlin but returned to Edinburgh where he worked for most of his medical career. He specialised in diseases of the eye and was eye surgeon at the Edinburgh Royal Infirmary and an ophthalmology lecturer at the University of Edinburgh. A tireless research worker, he made many lasting contributions in the field of eye conditions, diseases and treatments. It could truly be said of him that his name liveth forever more.

In Edinburgh he rapidly climbed the professional ladder and soon reached the top. He occupied the university chair of ophthalmology with distinction and his reputation rode high in all parts of the globe. His international fame drew the leading world figures of the day to his consulting room door, and he held the honorary appointment of eye physician to Queen Victoria, and Kind Edward VII.

It was in their respective roles as medical student and professor of ophthalmology that Grant first met Argyll Robertson. Grant, the

28 Dr Douglas Argyll Robertson

29 The Royal Infirmary of Edinburgh

95

undergraduate, demonstrated quite special ability, aptitude and interest in all matters related to the human eye. As he progressed through medical school this flair intensified and Lachlan Grant turned out to be one of the professor's top students. Indeed, in the final degree results in July 1893, Lachlan Grant was to share the first class honours prize in eye diseases with a fellow student, John Flett from Kirkwall. Grant went on to graduate with distinction and came under the wing of his 'Master.' By all accounts a good, respectful relationship built up and the young Dr Grant was detailed to assist Argyll Robertson in his hospital and clinic activities in and around Edinburgh. This was a prestigious position for any new graduate to hold, for it signalled likely professional advancement in the speciality. It was seen as a promise of better things to come, and the approval of the 'chief' was a useful passport to hold. The fact that Lachlan Grant forsook all that and chose instead a career in general practice, but still maintained a special friendship with the professor, is proof of the warmth of friendship and the respect they had for each other. One notes that at the time of the quarry dispute, the litigation that ensued, and the effort to raise the cost of expenses, Argyll Robertson was to chip in with a generous donation. Again, the friendship endured until the professor's death in 1909. In summary, it was a distinctive and distinguished friendship; not many like it

DR THOMAS SMITH CLOUSTON

Thomas Clouston was born in Orkney in 1840. He was educated on the island initially but transferred to Aberdeen's West End Academy (the Grammar School) to complete his schooling. From there he entered Edinburgh University Medical School and graduated in 1860, with MB, CM, and then an MD with Gold Medal in 1861. He served at Cumberland and Westmorland Asylum in Carlisle for ten years before being appointed head of the Edinburgh Royal Asylum in Morningside at the age of 33. In 1879 he became the first lecturer on mental diseases at Edinburgh University and he held the appointment until he retired in 1890.

30 Dr Thomas Smith Clouston

Clouston was thus lecturing and tutoring in psychiatry at the university when Lachlan

31 The Royal Edinburgh Asylum

Grant was a student there. The relationship of tutor-student developed through Grant's own interest in the subject and his aptitude for it. Grant was a diligent student and, once qualified, was selected by Dr Clouston to be house officer at his clinics in Edinburgh. At that point, and over his term of engagement as houseman, he found favour with Clouston and they became good friends. Though Clouston was eager to attract Grant into specialising in psychiatry, it transpired that the young doctor had set his heart on general practice. Nonetheless, Clouston made a big impression on Lachlan Grant.

Dr Clouston was an outstanding tutor and meticulous and disciplined doctor, who took detailed case histories of all his patients and was strict in the manner case-notes were recorded. He was also sensitive to the public reaction to mental diseases, and how patients were treated in the hands of clinicians. Clouston himself was masterful in both the clinical and diagnostic fields and the doyen of this speciality, not only in Edinburgh but far further afield. The university hierarchy held him in very high esteem and he cut a dash in all circles, in dress and deportment. Attired in a frock coat and striped trousers, he carried a silk hat and wore white gloves as he made his ward rounds each day, with a coterie of young graduate doctors in his wake.

Dr Clouston was a prolific writer who kept an eye on what appeared in the public press and kept cuttings of certain articles that caught his eye. He had a strong desire to raise public awareness of mental health and went out of his way to educate the public at large and improve their perceptions.

Making a detailed personal study of Thomas Clouston makes one realise how very nearly identical in their ways and manner he and Dr Grant were. There is much on record also to convince one that, if Dr Lachlan Grant ever wished to emulate any of his chiefs, Dr Thomas Clouston was the man. No wonder they made natural friends and shared a lasting friendship. No wonder too, that Dr Clouston was among the donors to the appeal fund during the quarries lockout in 1903, contributing one guinea, or £100 in today's currency.

Dr Thomas Clouston was deservedly knighted in 1911 and, most likely, Dr Lachlan Grant would have been one of the first colleagues to write to congratulate him on his award. Thomas Clouston died in 1915 at the age of 75 years.

DR ROGER McNEILL
FIRST MEDICAL OFFICER OF HEALTH FOR ARGYLLSHIRE

Roger McNeill, the son of a crofter, was born in 1853 at Ardskenish, on Colonsay – the 'lonely isle.' His real Christian name was Ruairidh but the name became sadly anglicised to Roger when he left his native home for his secondary education and that name took hold. He was nevertheless a fluent Gaelic speaker, who was recognised even in his early years to be of formidable and brilliant intellect. He was the youngest of 11 children and, when his mother died at their home in Colonsay in 1859, Roger was a mere six years old. At that time there was no resident doctor on the island, and he witnessed his mother die without access to medical services. The event was to enter his soul; it forever influenced him in all his deeds and life's work.

32 Dr Roger McNeill

His choice of career and profession was therefore unsurprising. He enrolled at Edinburgh University Medical School in 1872, aged nineteen. His colleagues said of him that no student ever entered medicine with finer motive than Roger McNeill, and no doctor ever practised in the profession, so honest a man. He was humble and modest and left it to others to sound trumpet. At medical school McNeill shone academically, graduating MB, MS in 1877, progressing to MD Gold Medal with first class honours in 1881, and a DPH from the University of Cambridge in 1889. Post-graduation, he worked intensively in Manchester and in London, gaining a wealth of medical experience in treating and containing infectious and communicable diseases. In 1883 the trustees of the Gesto Hospital in Skye appointed him as its resident medical officer, five years after the hospital opened, and he remained in that gruelling position until 1890, when he became the first appointed Medical Officer of Health for Argyllshire. As MOH, he gave distinguished service to that county and its people. He held the post until his death in 1924 and, though his career in public health was illustrious, it was massively understated on account of his personal modesty. Torrents of gracious tributes, however, were heaped upon him following his death, and the end of his professional labours. He was quietly laid to rest back in his native island, lulled by the sough of the sea. His simple gravestone on Colonsay is inscribed with a plain message:

'In loving memory of Roger McNeill MD, DPH, JP, County Medical Officer of Argyll 1890-1924.
Born at Colonsay 15th April 1853. Died at Edinburgh 16th April 1924.
Psalm 54: v 3'

Though Roger McNeill was twenty-eight years senior to Lachlan Grant, who was born in the same year as McNeill graduated, their working lives became close when, from 1900, Dr Grant was the local MO and MOH at Ballachulish and Dr McNeill was County Officer of Health in Oban. The two men shared a common culture, enjoyed similar student successes, served as resident medical officers, separately, at Gesto, and returned to their native Argyll to serve the greater part of their career; they also held a common outlook, the same belief and ethos. They worked closely and effectively together on all public health matters, as affected 'their people' and both were to the fore in serving such interests. They were in the front rank of their profession and, on Roger McNeill's death in 1924, his good friend and trusted colleague had this to say: 'Up to the last he was zealous and active in his appointed work. He was painstakingly accurate and conscientious in carrying out his public duties. He will be remembered as a pioneer and as an example to those who follow in his footsteps.'

There is all the evidence to suggest that their friendship was forged through the aims and the ambitions they held, and hoped for others to attain. Honourable men, both.

DR WILLIAM MURDIE

Dr William Murdie was a native of West Sutherlandshire, the son of Mr and Mrs Alexander Murdie of Stronchrubie, a small hamlet at the head of Loch Assynt, near Inchnadamph. He was educated at Edinburgh University, where he graduated MB, ChB in 1907. For many years he served as locum and assistant to Dr Grant at Ballachulish, caring particularly for the patients in Kinlochleven. He and Dr Grant enjoyed a good professional relationship and forged a firm personal friendship. When Dr Grant married in 1915, in Edinburgh, he chose Dr Murdie to be his best man.

33 Dr William Murdie and Dr Grant

Like Grant, he contributed much to medical literature with papers published in the medical press on vaccines in general practice, observations on infection by the tubercle bacillus and a case of camphor poisoning. Some of these contributions were prepared and published jointly with Dr Grant and they both teamed up to invent the aluminium throat swab in 1913.

In his later years Dr Murdie lived and worked in the north-east of England, being appointed the medical officer and public vaccinator for the 5th District of Bellingham and as medical officer to the Post Office. He lived at Wark-on-Tyne and was sadly killed in an accident there on 31 July 1941. Dr Grant held him in high esteem both as a professional assistant and trusted, personal friend.

PROF. ARCHIBALD YOUNG

Professor Archibald Young was Glasgow-born, Glasgow-educated, Glasgow-trained and lived and worked in the city for most of his life. Born in 1873, he was virtually co-ages with Lachlan Grant. Young received his education at Glasgow High School and Glasgow University Medical School, from which he graduated BSc in 1893, and MB, CM with high commendation in 1895. As was common then, he spent some period of study at the European centres of excellence of the time, namely Berlin, Breslau and Heidelberg. On return to Glasgow, he rose through the surgical ranks, assisting eminent doyens like Prof Joseph Coats, and Sir William MacEwen. Gaining his FRFPS in 1913, he was appointed Professor of Surgery

34 Professor Archibald Young

at the Anderson College of Medicine, Glasgow. During World War 1 he worked as a neurologist at No. 4 Scottish General Hospital, and was appointed visiting surgeon at the Western Infirmary in Glasgow. In 1924 came his appointment to the Regius Chair of Surgery at Glasgow University, which he held until his untimely and unexpected death in 1939, at the age of 65 years.

In 1900, when Dr Grant was appointed MO to Ballachulish, Glasgow was the nearest centre to which one could refer patients for hospital care and opinion. In this way close ties built up between GPs and the hospital consultants. Being of the same 'vintage,' it is fair to accept that close contact at professional level would lead to personal friendship, as was indeed the case with Dr Grant and Prof Young. Their relationship stretched from 1900 to 1939. Dr Grant was to outlive Dr Young by six years. The professor's death must have been a great personal and professional blow to Dr Grant and his patients. His services were highly valued. Prof Young was particularly skilled at operative treatment of fractures and at pain relief methods.

The many friends of Prof Young, Dr Grant among them, were set to mark his retirement by commissioning his portrait in oils. Subscriptions had been solicited but the plans had to be hurriedly advanced when news of his terminal illness emerged. To everyone's great relief, however, the gift materialised in good time before his demise, thus friends and colleagues marked the occasion of retirement and death of their special friend and colleague within a very short space of time.

Professor Young was a straightforward, modest man of towering talent, meticulous and diligent in all his undertakings. He was loyal to his colleagues and kind to his patients. It was little wonder his friendships were firm, and lasted long.

SIR JOHN FRASER

The son of a Tain farmer, John Fraser's roots were firmly fixed in Easter Ross. His brilliant mind, however, diverted him from family farming activity and set him out on the academic path. There are certain parallels to his early life and that of Lachlan Grant. Though Fraser was 14 years junior to Grant, both shared an Easter Ross connection, both studied at Edinburgh University Medical School and both enjoyed a dazzling student career there. John Fraser graduated with honours in 1907 and gained the class medal in clinical surgery. His reputation, at an early stage in his career, was established in his research on bone and joint tuberculosis in children. The First World War interrupted his plans, but he served with distinction in the Royal Army Medical Corps. He was wounded in 1916 and awarded the Military Cross. Subsequently, a return to civilian surgery saw him pioneer heart surgery, becoming the first surgeon in Scotland to undertake 'hole in the heart' vascular surgery. In 1927 he succeeded to the prestigious Chair of Clinical Surgery in Edinburgh and was knighted in 1937.

He was known as an inspiring teacher, a superb diagnostician and an impressive operating surgeon. Throughout his life he was a person to cultivate good relationships with professional friends and colleagues, and they in turn respectfully sought his opinion and services for patient care. Dr Grant, in a long medical career, thus ranked John Fraser among his working colleagues and he much relied on his surgical skills. Besides, they forged a firm enduring friendship. Sir John Fraser was to meet his untimely death in 1947, only two years after Dr Grant himself had passed away.

DR. THE REV. THOMAS MOFFAT MURCHISON

Born in Glasgow in 1907, Thomas Moffat Murchison moved with his family to the Isle of Skye when he was 6 years of age. He grew up on the island in a crofting community, and lived the life of a crofter's son. He was 36 years younger than Dr Grant and, at that, would seem to belong to another generation. Yet they became bosom buddies. They formed an amazingly effective partnership to pursue measures that would improve the Highlands and Islands in general, and the lot of the Gaels in particular.

Murchison was highly intelligent and scholarly. He was a theologian, a renowned preacher, a great Gaelic scholar, a broadcaster and an editor. A graduate of Glasgow University, he gained MA, DD degrees and began ministry in Glenelg in 1932. He had extensive knowledge of the Highlands and Islands, and of Skye and Glenelg especially. Tom Murchison served as a councillor on Inverness County Council while in Glenelg. In the early 1930s he teamed up with Dr Lachlan Grant to establish himself as an ardent advocate on Highland issues. They joined forces within many of the organisations founded for the pursuit of such laudable aims as, for example, those of the Sea League (1933), the New Deal (1934), the Development League (1936), the Skye

35 The Rev Dr T.M. Murchison

Crofters' Association (1938), and so on. Preservation and advancement of the Gaelic language and culture was also of shared concern.

The Rev Thomas Murchison left Glenelg in 1937 to take up the charge of St Columba's Copland Road, in Govan. Despite his move to the city, Tom Murchison did not lose touch with his friend. He and Dr Grant continued their campaigning together, right up to the time of Dr Grant's death in 1945 and after, with Murchison continuing to fight the good fight until his own demise in 1984.

The efforts and achievements of both men were enormous although many of Murchison's own aims and achievements were secured in the years between 1945 and 1984. It was fitting that the Rev Tom Murchison officiated at Dr Grant's funeral service at Craigleven and at the graveside at Duror in 1945. They were stout friends and their hearts beat as one.

JOHN MACDONALD BANNERMAN (JMB)

Through their many common interests – political, social, cultural and historical – it is no surprise that Johnnie Bannerman ranked as one of Dr Grant's best friends. Hardly a platform existed in the Highlands or in Glasgow that they did not grace in consort or in concert! Though he was born in Glasgow, Bannerman's roots went back to South Uist, on his father's side, and he was a proud, fluent Gaelic speaker himself in his many roles. His sporting prowess in rugby, as a forward for Glasgow and Oxford Universities RFC, 'rugby blue' from Oxford and 37 caps for Scotland in the years 1921 to 1929, hugely added to his charisma. Born in 1901, he was 30 younger than Lachlan Grant. It was their parallel, deep interest in Highland affairs and in the welfare of the Gaels that bound them in such common purpose. Dr Grant was a known Liberal, locally and in and around Argyll where he was President of the Liberal Association. JMB was a dyed-in-the-wool Liberal, his name synonymous with the cause, so there was nothing at all to divide them on ideology nor on the numerous issues they were bent on driving forward in the interests of the Gaidhealtachd: emigration, land use, the fishing industry, promotion of industry and employment in the Highlands, social welfare issues, and (naturally) the language and culture of the Gael. While Lachlan Grant had powerful views and ideas in these matters, Johnnie Bannerman was no less formidable an advocate of their common concerns. He had ample achievement to his name with academic qualifications from

36 John Bannerman

Glasgow, Oxford and Cornell Universities, and hands-on experience in farming, forestry and land management. He was factor to the Duke of Montrose, and farmed on his own account. He was power to Dr Grant's elbow and on a public platform the one complemented the other. Among the Gaelic fraternity both men were greatly respected. Ceilidhs, especially among Glasgow Highlanders, were a lively affair and a palatable blend of entertainment, oratory and the airing and advancement of political ideas. It raised morale too, to have Mrs Grant on stage to sing classical Gaelic songs. Bannerman loved nothing better than to go on stage to entertain in Gaelic song and voice.

As with all his friends, Dr Grant communicated freely and frequently by letter. Correspondence between him and Bannerman is delightful. On one particular occasion, when Dr Grant sent a copy of his pamphlet entitled 'Ten Commandments of Health,' Bannerman replied in Gaelic, in his unique handwriting of 'curls and cromags.' Even in translation to English, this is vintage Bannerman. Writing from his home in Gourock on 22.6.1935, he responded thus:

'My kind and beloved friend,

We are much indebted to you for your letters and books and the pleasant things from which we drink goodness and which from time to time you send us. Believe me that I read with sincerity every advice you give me, as I am very often of the same mind as you, regarding the things our people must to take to heart, if they wish to live long and succeed in the world as Gaels. I wish you every success, and also your household, and at the Mod.

    With compliments to all,

    Kind regards. 'Fear na Brataich' (Bannerman)'

It is plain to see why Johnnie Bannerman was a friend to many, and an enemy of none. His long friendship with Lachlan Grant was in itself a positive power for the good.

THOMAS 'TOM' JOHNSTON
SECRETARY OF STATE FOR SCOTLAND

Tom Johnston was a grocer's son from Kirkintilloch, who received his education at Lenzie Academy and Glasgow University. Born in 1881, he was 10 years younger than Dr Grant. Johnston had close associations with the Red Clydesiders. He first entered Parliament in 1922 (Stirling & Clackmannan), lost the seat in 1924, but returned to Westminster that same year via a Dundee by-election. After the 1929 general election he was appointed Under Secretary of State for Scotland by the Prime Minister, Ramsay MacDonald. He had considerable disagreements with MacDonald; indeed they fell out spectacularly. It was, however, his contribution to government in his wartime roles, from 1939 onwards, that earned him his remarkable reputation in Scotland. Churchill appointed him Secretary of State for Scotland in 1941, which post he held till 1945. In many people's view, Johnston was a giant figure in Scottish politics and he is revered to this day as the greatest Scottish Secretary of the century. His initiatives to promote Scotland were numerous and intrinsically of great merit and benefit to the country, and the Highlands in particular. His creation of the North of Scotland Hydro-Electric Board was his single greatest legacy. It is no wonder Dr Grant focused his attention on Johnston and quickly recognised in him the ability to deliver in government. From 1929, Grant gained his confidence and sent him detailed briefings on a regular basis as to what the Highland problems were and what the solutions had to be. When one scans the list of Tom Johnston's achievements throughout the Highlands – and they were many – one can spot the connection between them and Dr

Grant's numerous campaigns on behalf of Highlanders. It is a remarkable parallel. When Dr Grant's Golden Jubilee in general practice was celebrated at a luncheon in Oban in November 1944, the doctor was showered with numerous tributes from colleagues, friends and patients. One tribute was noted above all the others, that from Tom Johnston, the Secretary of State for Scotland. It was prefaced by an apology for not being present in person due to pressure or government business, but the tribute Johnston paid to the doctor was generous in praise 'for what Dr Grant has done for the Highlands and Islands.' It was genuine, sincere and deserved; a tribute that was truly the salute of one good friend to another.

Dr Grant died the following May (1945), and Tom Johnston was among the first to tender his condolences; he had lost a trusted, reliable friend who, like Johnston himself, always had the Highlands at heart. It was such a shame that Dr Grant did not live to see 'TJ' go on to greater glory in his achievements as chairman of the Scottish National Forestry Commission (1945-48) and the North of Scotland Hydro-Electric Board (1946-59), and Chancellor of Aberdeen University from 1951 until his death in 1965.

COMPTON MACKENZIE ('MONTY')

Compton MacKenzie was an exquisite type of character and hugely loved, in the Islands and Highlands in particular. It pained him to have been born in West Hartlepool, south of the Border, and it grieved him that his father had gone out of his way to discard the old family surname of MacKenzie for the English-sounding surname of Compton. It became his priority to redress the balance and, at the earliest possible moment, restored his MacKenzie surname and refashioned his Scottish roots. To this end, he took himself north to Scotland, donned the kilt as his garb and lived, variously, in rented houses such as the schoolhouse in north Barra, or on rented

37 Compton Mackenzie

islands such as Eilean Aigas near Beauly. In retracing his Highland ancestry he became an enthusiast of the Gaelic language, the Gaelic culture and the Gaelic people. He became an ardent Jacobite, a founder member of the Scottish Nationalist Party, converted to Catholicism (1914) and was elected as Rector of Glasgow University (1931-1934). When he completed this rehabilitation, he very effectively took on the role of political activist. He built a house in Barra and set up home there in 1930, forging a close relationship with the islanders who adored him. He took up political issues that concerned them and, as he loved to cross swords with politicians, civil servants and the mandarins at Westminster and the Scottish Office, he accepted the challenge with relish! It was in this capacity that he linked into Dr Grant's campaign on land reform, on employment, coastal fishing issues and so forth. It was a two-way relationship in that Dr Grant and his 'buddy' the Rev Tom Murchison of Glenelg were delighted to give their support to MacKenzie in establishing the Sea League in 1933. Compton MacKenzie travelled around the Highlands and Islands far more extensively than people realise. His celebrated persona apart, he relied on his staunch Catholic faith to gain the confidence and respect of local priests and so developed a network of 'safe houses' to live in wherever he went in the predominantly Catholic parts of the Highlands, the Islands, Lochaber and Argyll. Chapel houses there were open to him, and Highland priests entertained him, being famously discreet and hospitable to a man. On occasions such as these, he visited Dr Grant at Craigleven to ceilidh, discuss and do political business. Hospitality there was made easy with Mrs Grant's fine cooking and great Gaelic singing, and Dr Grant accompanying her on the piano. In my own early days in Ballachulish the older priests confided in me how discreet a 'plan' it was, and how much fun resulted. On such visits MacKenzie, with his keen, observant eye, gleaned a great deal about the people, culture and the politics of Gaeldom. There was exchange of written correspondence and the concise, neatly hand-written letters from 'Monty' are among Dr Grant's own collected journals. Dr Grant was of course not slow to post to him a copy of the many pamphlets he wrote! One reply received from Compton MacKenzie to such a gift, is most engaging. Dr Grant had sent him his pamphlet titled 'Napoleon the Great.' The acknowledgement from Monty at Eilean Aigas, Beauly, Inverness-shire, on 4 Nov 1931, read as follows:

Dear Doctor,
Many thanks for your letter, and for your interesting lecture on Napoleon. You chose a large subject and managed to treat it with wonderful conciseness.
All kind regards to Mrs Grant and your family.
Yours sincerely,
Compton MacKenzie

In matters of personal friendship and human relationship one senses that MacKenzie was a most kindly man, sensitive, respectful and very discreet.

JOHN LORNE CAMPBELL
('FEAR CHANAIDH')

John Lorne Campbell was a curious man who seemed to inhabit a world of his own, and it is said that, owing to his shy and prickly nature, he experienced difficulty in dealing with people. Yet he immersed himself in Gaelic anthology, the songs of the '45 and the folklore of South Uist and Barra, enjoying a warm friendship with these islanders. Along with his wife Fay, an American musicologist, he collected, captured and archived many of the Gaelic songs and the oral traditions which were

38 John Lorne Campbell

on the point of extinction in these islands. He lived on Barra in the 1930s and there enjoyed a close friendship with Compton MacKenzie, with whom he founded the Sea League in 1933. It was this event in particular that was to draw him together with Dr Grant. They had a shared concern over the welfare of the west coast fishermen and their families, and the organisation they founded was intended to stir government officials to protect the islanders' livelihood.

It seems clear that they also shared certain opinions and beliefs that were 'core' in value. For example, when John Lorne Campbell wrote the following lines they could have just as readily flowed from the pen of Dr Lachlan Grant: 'I felt strongly that the Highlanders had too often put their loyalty unreservedly at the disposal of Westminster governments, which in peacetime had promptly forgotten their services, and had in times past tolerated the evictions and clearances which had torn thousands from their homes and had shown subsequent neglect which resulted in the Highlands and Islands being the poorest and most backward part of the country.' They shared common values, and the friendship between them was a pragmatic working arrangement rather than a purely emotional one. As Campbell was descended from a family of minor landowning Argyll aristocrats, Grant may have been wary of him, knowing the icy emotions that could at times emanate from members of this class. Whatever part personality may have played, one thing is for sure: on Sea League issues they were united as one. There was nothing fickle about it.

ARCHIBALD SINCLAIR (1st VISCOUNT THURSO)

Archie Sinclair was a Liberal politician of aristocratic background. Educated at Eton and RMA Sandhurst, he was commissioned into the Life Guards in 1910, served on the Western Front during the First World War and served as second-in-command to Winston Churchill, when he commanded 6th Bn, The Royal Scots Fusiliers in 1916. He enjoyed excellent relations with Churchill both in the army and in politics. Sinclair represented the northern Highland seat of Caithness & Sutherland from 1922-1945 and was leader of the Liberal Party from 1935-1945. He served Ramsay MacDonald as Secretary of State for Scotland from 1931 to 1932 and Churchill as Secretary of State for Air from 1940 to 1945. As a long-serving Highland MP for one of the largest and most rural of parliamentary seats, and as a Liberal,

39 Archibald Sinclair, Viscount Thurso

he was held in some regard by Dr Grant with whom he shared and discussed the problems of the Highlands. They exchanged political correspondence, especially over the Caledonian Power Scheme. There was concern in many quarters that the flooding of scenic parts of the north by the building of hydro-electric dams would place the Highlands under water. There was a grave risk that failure to pass the CPS Bill would put an end to electricity generation schemes in the Highlands. Dr Grant, of course, would have none of this and he pressed on furiously and ever harder to bring this 'much-needed and suitable industry' to the rural Highland area. In 1937 this issue generated volumes of correspondence between the two individuals, and served to strengthen their relationship and resolve.

Sinclair was considered to be handsome and charming, but he was shy and reserved and had a speech impediment. For all that, his dealings with Dr Grant were cordial, good-natured and purposeful.

DONALD THOMAS ROSE ('DT ROSE')

Donald Thomas Rose, or 'DT Rose' as he signed his artwork, became well recognised and regarded in the art world and among art lovers. He was an interesting man, born in 1871 in the Scottish Borders and brought up in Nairn,

The navvy

The ganger

40 DT Rose sketches

Work on a side cutting

Hand drilling

where his father ran the family butchery business. He was co-ages with Dr Grant but they did not meet one another till later in life.

Rose trained as a civil engineer and his time in Glasgow (1896) stirred his interest in art and in the work of the Glasgow Boys, especially Arthur Melville (1855-1904). From 1896 to 1898 Rose studied at night classes at the Glasgow School of Art and took his talent to a professional level.

It was in his capacity as an engineer, however, that he found his way back to Argyllshire. He was engaged in the construction of the Callander & Oban Railway Line, from Connel Ferry to Ballachulish, between 1896 and 1903. While living in the area over that period he was to make the acquaintance of Lachlan Grant, the newly-appointed GP at Ballachulish. Grant was then 29 years old, the same age as Rose. They became firm friends in the three years remaining till Rose completed the project. Interestingly, and likely as a token of friendship, Rose gave Grant a couple of his original art works, dated 1901 and signed by the artist. Contact continued and in 1904, another original piece was gifted to the doctor. Donald Rose paid return visits to the area for many years, after the time of Dr Grant's marriage in 1915 and later after the birth of his three daughters, the point being that DT Rose sketched drawings for the Grant girls and tutored them in art. The DT Rose friendship, which started with Dr Grant alone, flourished to become one embracing the whole family. Donald Rose died in 1964, outliving his friend by nigh on 29 years.

Incidentally, the Rose art work has been graciously returned to Craigleven, at the behest of Mrs Sheena Roddan, Dr Grant's eldest daughter, who felt it had 'its proper home' there.

JAMES RAMSAY MACDONALD (JRM) *(See plate 26, page 87)*

Ramsay MacDonald hailed from Morayshire and remained rooted in that part of the north east, being immensely proud of it. He was born in Lossiemouth and brought up there by his mother. Little is said or known about his father. Be that as it may, MacDonald was a most resilient figure whose career in journalism and trade unionism led to his election to the United Kingdom Parliament. Once into active national politics he attained the ultimate prize in that profession: the office of Prime Minister. He served firstly as Prime Minister and leader of a Labour Government for just less than one year, January 1924 to November 1924. A spell in Opposition followed while Stanley Baldwin led the nation as the Conservative Prime Minister; in 1929, MacDonald returned to head a Labour Government, continuing in 1931 as head of a coalition Government until 1935. There is no doubt Ramsay MacDonald found his latter years in office very stressful and tiring. The Labour Party had lost confidence in him. But it was between the 1920s and 1930s that he and Dr Lachlan Grant communicated extensively and became good personal friends. Many people in the north of Scotland know of that friendship and connection, but very few realise how close a relationship it was and how it also embraced other members of both families. Ramsay MacDonald became a frequent visitor to Craigleven and it afforded him a 'pit stop' as he travelled north from London to his home in Lossiemouth, and, likewise on his return journey south. He would alert the Grants a few weeks in advance of his intention to visit, and it seems, on arrival, would make a beeline for the open fireplace. There, before its blazing presence, standing in his plus fours suit, he would take a dram in his hand and eagerly engage in conversation. Of those occasions Mrs Roddan recalls that, as young girls, she and her sisters never forgot the smell of burning tweed!

There was never any shortage of issues to cover and, as the letters they exchanged reveal, there was the utmost mutual trust and confidence in the relationship. Ramsay MacDonald paid careful attention to Mrs Grant, her health on occasion, her singing success at the Gaelic Mods and the progress of their three daughters. They exchanged personal gifts as occasion demanded and every Christmas and New Year exchanged greetings of the season. Hospitality was not one way, as Dr and Mrs Grant were from time to time invited to luncheon at No. 10 Downing Street and entertained there. His daughter, Ishbel, often acted as his hostess and attended to the needs of their invited guests. She and Mrs Grant became firm friends and they too exchanged their own personal messages.

On examination, it is not clear what political gain, if any, there was for either Grant or MacDonald in the relationship. Their briefing of one another may have had value, and kept them both informed on the issues of the moment in the Highlands and Islands. Being of a romantic nature and a MacDonald, the PM found proximity to Glencoe a nostalgic experience. Grant, for his part, possessed inquisitiveness into the workings of government.

Ramsay MacDonald was widowed for a long period. He had six children, of whom Ishbel and his son Malcolm (elected for the MP for Ross and Cromarty in 1936) have already been mentioned. They were all close to their parents and cared for their father in his frail state after he left office. It was certainly with sadness in their hearts that Dr and Mrs Grant learnt of their friend's death on 9 November 1937, while on a holiday cruise to South America. MacDonald's body was embalmed in the Bahamas, then flown home and laid to rest beside his late wife at Spynie Cemetery in his beloved Morayshire. He was 71 years of age.

The following letters from the Grant family archive serve to paint a picture of a personal and touching friendship: maybe surpassing one's expectations, given their different political allegiances.

July 16th 1923

My dear Grant

Thank you very much for yours of the 12th.

I am quite with you that the great balance is in favour of the Insurance Act. There have been cases of neglect where doctors have shown no public spirit, but these have been exceptions and, they would soon be weeded out. I am sending your letter with your Journal to our Public Health Committee.

One day, about the 16th September, I will knock at your door and see if you are in – provided the present plans I am making will come off. I propose to start from Glasgow by motor on Saturday, the 15th, and I hope to come down to Glencoe on Sunday, the 16th.

With kindest regards

Yours sincerely

JRM

June 17th 1925

Private & Confidential

My dear Grant

Thank you very much for your virile pamphlet and more particularly for the photograph of your two young folks. They are a great advertisement for the health and beauty that one can pick up amongst your hills. I was in Scotland a few days ago and I have never seen it better. The broom and the whins were out together, and it was a terrible wrench to come back here.

You tell a sad tale of the quarries. I do not know what is overtaking us. We seem to have no energy, and no enterprise left, but are rushing behind brick walls and into ditches for safety. I sometimes get very dissatisfied with the vast amount of pandering that is being done in our Labour Movement. Instead of preaching energy to do one's best and then to claim a just reward, we are dwelling, I sometimes think, far too much upon assistance from outside, and doles.

Yours very sincerely,

JRM

25th May 1929

Oban Times Report:

The Rt Hon James Ramsay MacDonald, ex-Premier, in his political tour through the Highlands after addressing a meeting at Fort William, motored to Ballachulish Ferry through the Cameron country, and passed through Ballachulish and called on Dr Grant JP, thereafter proceeding through the historic and romantic Glencoe, where the new road is being constructed to Oban. It would be with mixed feelings that Mr MacDonald would pass the scene of the Massacre of Glencoe, where his kinsmen were massacred in 1692.

Letter from Miss Ishbel MacDonald to Mrs Catherine Grant

Hillocks
Lossiemouth
Scotland
23rd December 1932

Dear Mrs Grant

Very many thanks for the sweet coffee cups you have so kindly sent me. We shall use them tonight. They come as a very pleasant surprise.

Lossiemouth has done my father good. He was very tired before he came here; but unfortunately I cannot cut off the telephone or prevent work from reaching him.

I hope you will all have a very happy Christmas and New Year and that by January 2nd it will be impossible for any of you to think of trying to get through the pillars in the cabinet room.

Again thanking you.

Yours sincerely
Ishbel MacDonald

10

Tributes to Tenacity

Throughout his professional life many tributes and accolades were paid to Lachlan Grant. These originated from medical and lay sources alike and from leaders of organisations he helped, founded and supported. The personal tributes paid to him in his early days by the Skye crofters, at the time he left Gesto Hospital to take up appointment at the Ballachulish Slate Quarries, really rank among the kindest and most sincere compliments possible. While his service to people was appreciated throughout his fifty years in medicine, it was towards the end of his career, at his Jubilee celebration in 1944, at the time of his retirement in 1945, and ultimately on his death in 1945, that the full chorus of praise was raised. It seems appropriate for us to draw on a selection of these contributions, adding them to all the praises that already pepper this narrative of his rich and varied life.

TRIBUTE by The Rev THOMAS M. MURCHISON M.A D.D
In 1936 the Rev Thomas Tom Murchison paid a handsome tribute to Dr Grant in the pages of the *Northern Times*. 'It requires but a bold spirit,' he said, 'to tackle problems. Dr Lachlan Grant, Ballachulish, is a pioneer in a thousand. His heart is in the Highland problems, and if anything can be done in his life-time to bring about better times for the Highland people, he will accomplish it.' Informing the public at large of his admiration for Dr Grant, the Rev Murchison continued: 'I admire people of the pioneering spirit of Dr Grant. They are a valuable asset to any country or community.'

TRIBUTE by *THE SCOTSMAN*, Editorial, 1 June 1945
The late Lachlan Grant – Founder of the Highland Development League 'Dr Grant came to prominence in the early 1930s through his agitation for High-land development. He was the author of 'New Deal for the Highlands.' The League, which he originated, spread rapidly, and included branches in Edinburgh and Glasgow. These initiated discussion on Highland problems and sought to arouse the interest of MPs of all parties. After a few years of these activities, Dr

Grant, dissatisfied with the result, joined the Scottish National Party.'

TRIBUTE by AN ACADEMIC FRIEND, TO DR GRANT:
'He dipped deeply in to the classics and made himself thoroughly conversant with the Masters of English literature...'

TRIBUTE by Rt. Hon. TOM JOHNSTON M.P., Secretary of State for Scotland
'You have given long and distinguished service to the common folk of your country and you have created a reputation for good works in the Highlands that will long outlive your day and generation.'

THE CAMANACHD ASSOCIATION:
'A generous supporter of the game of shinty, and other sports, and was for the last forty years Chief of the Ballachulish Camanachd Club.'

TRIBUTE by THE LOCAL PRESS, following the Jubilee Luncheon in November 1944:
Dr Lachlan Grant completed 50 years in the medical profession in August 1944 and, officially, this was his Golden Jubilee date. His medical colleagues decided to hold a celebratory luncheon in Oban in November that year, to mark the occasion. By all accounts it was a splendid affair and the local press gave it good coverage. The news report published at the time, in 1944, is shown opposite:

Memorials Created to the Memory of Dr Lachlan Grant (1871–1945)

While many fine tributes were paid to Dr Lachlan Grant following his death on 31 May 1945, by many people from all walks of life and from near and far, the tone was certainly set by the plain, simple and well-written obituary which appeared in the *British Medical Journal* on 16 June 1945. It was carefully crafted and composed by a former GP who served the Ballachulish community from 1889 to 1892, and who had got to know Lachlan Grant then as a 'young boy of 18 years.' As a précis of his professional life the tribute is as concise and complete as one would wish. The obituary in full, by the late Dr James Bertie

BALLACHULISH

A DISTINGUISHED MEDICAL PRACTITIONER

MANY FRIENDS WILL BE PLEASED TO HEAR that Dr Lachlan Grant, Ballachulish, has celebrated his jubilee as a medical practitioner. Dr Grant has done great work for the Highlands and Islands as a skilful physician, as the author of "The New Deal for the Highlands" and as an accomplished speaker and lecturer and writer of distinction.

He was born at Johnstone, where his father, who was a native of Wester Ross, was engaged in business. His maternal grandfather was Mr Wm. Paton, manufacturer, Johnstone Mill, a gentleman who was well known and much respected in business circles in the West of Scotland. While Dr Grant was still young, the family removed to Ballachulish, and it was in the public school there that he received the elements of his education. In 1889 he was enrolled as a medical student in Edinburgh University. In 1894 he graduated M.B., C.M. With a view to further equipping himself for his life's work, he studied mental disease under Dr Clouston of Morningside Asylum, and subsequently became assistant to Dr Argyll Robertson.

In 1896 he was appointed assistant to Dr McCalman, Oban. Later he was appointed medical officer to the Gesto Hospital in Skye. From Skye he went to Ballachulish in 1900. Shortly afterwards it was written of him that "By his skill and kindness, and by the uprightness of his character, he soon gained for himself the esteem and confidence, and it may be added, the affection of the entire community." In the four and forty years of his work in Ballachulish he has kept abreast of the latest discoveries in his profession and to-day his many accomplishments are known and appreciated throughout Scotland.

He started a bacteriological laboratory serving the Lorn District and adjacent District Committee of Inverness.

In 1921 he was elected a member of the Royal Faculty of Physicians and Surgeons of Glasgow. Of all the congratulations reaching him at this time, the tribute that is likely to attract most attention is the one from Mr Thomas Johnston, Secretary of State for Scotland, who is generous in his praise of what Dr Grant has done for the Highlands and Islands.

Mrs Grant, the talented wife of Dr Grant, is one of the sweetest singers of our time. At the Mod Festivals she won chief prizes, and has been lavish in her help of entertainments for charitable purposes from near and far. The daughters of Dr Grant and Mrs Grant are busy helping in the national effort.

41 'A Distinguished Medical Practitioner', November 1944

Simpson of Golspie, is a masterpiece of its kind:

'Dr Lachlan Grant, who died at his home at Ballachulish, Argyll, on May 31, was one of the most senior medical officers in the Highlands and Islands Medical Service. He spent all of his professional life (over 50 years) in the Highlands, and acquired a wonderful knowledge of Highland problems as they affected the Highland people. The writer of these notes was one of Dr Grant's predecessors in Ballachulish in 1889-92. Lachlan Grant, whose home was then in Ballachulish, was a boy of 18. A friendship followed our first meeting, and soon after, the boy told me that he wished to become 'a doctor' if his father would permit him to remain in the Highlands and practise among the people. He chose Edinburgh University, and in 1894 graduated MB, CM (with distinction), and MD in 1896, took DPH in 1911, and later FRFPS Glasgow. The prosperity of Ballachulish in those far-off days depended entirely on the flourishing slate quarries. A large number of men were employed on the 'slate face.' The men were an exceptionally fine type physically. They were intelligent and interested not only in slate quarrying as an art but in political problems connected with the Highlands. Lachlan Grant was not only a 'good doctor' for them and their wives and children, he was also interested, they recognised, in Highland problems. And so it was that during his 50 years' service in Ballachulish, Glencoe, Kinlochleven, and Glenetive, and the rest of that wonderful and historic piece of country, Lachlan Grant was the man to whom the people turned in adversity, for he was not only a skilful physician but a sympathetic friend and adviser. Ballachulish mourns his loss. To his devoted wife and family we offer our sympathy.

J.B.S.'

Dr. James B. Simpson
Golspie

Being the widely respected figure he had become, it was inevitable that on his death, vast coverage was given to his memory in the local, national and medical press. After all, in his own long life, Dr Grant had contributed, and generated, many acres of newsprint in the same publications! Typical of the tributes paid to him was the one featured in *The Oban Times* of 31 May 1945, and is worth recalling not just as a tribute, but of the effect news of his death had within the Argyllshire community:

'The late Dr Lachlan Grant, Ballachulish: Prominent in Medicine and

Research. It is with deep regret that we record the death, after a short illness, of Dr Lachlan Grant, on Thursday evening, May 31, at his residence, Craigleven, Ballachulish. He was the eldest son of the late Mr Peter Grant and the late Mrs Grant, who were known in business and social circles. Dr Grant received the elements of his education in Ballachulish Public School, and in 1889 was enrolled as a medical student in Edinburgh University, where he graduated in 1894, MB, CM. He studied mental diseases under Dr Clouston in Morningside Asylum, Edinburgh. Subsequently, he became assistant to Dr Argyll Robertson, Royal Infirmary, Edinburgh, and in 1896 he was appointed assistant to Dr MacCalman, Oban. Afterwards he was selected medical officer to Gesto Hospital, Edinbane, Isle of Skye.

In August 1900, he went to Ballachulish where by his skill and kindness, and by the uprightness of his character, he soon gained for himself the esteem and confidence and affection of the whole community. In the 45 years of his work in Ballachulish and the surrounding district he kept abreast of the latest discoveries of his profession, and his many accomplishments were well known and appreciated not only in the Highlands, but throughout Scotland.

In 1921 he was made a Fellow of the Royal Faculty of Physicians and Surgeons in Glasgow in virtue of distinction in Medical Science and Practice. He also held the Diploma of Public Health and was a Justice of the Peace for Argyll. Dr Grant was a writer of distinction, an accomplished speaker and lecturer, and prominent in medicine and research. Beside the important industrial town of Kinlochleven, he had also charge of the Glencoe Auxiliary Hospital.

In celebration of his attaining his jubilee as a medical practitioner he was, last November, the honoured guest of members of the medical profession at a luncheon held in Oban, when he received gifts of a silver Quaich and a wallet of notes, and Mrs Grant a gold bracelet. Of all the tributes paid to Dr Grant at that time, perhaps the most outstanding was from Mr Thomas Johnston, the then Secretary of State for Scotland.

Dr Grant was a generous supporter of the game of shinty and other sports, and was for the last 40 years Chief of the Ballachulish Camanachd Club.

His passing is a distinct loss, not only to Ballachulish and surrounding district, but to the Highlands generally. Much sympathy has been extended to Mrs Grant and family of three daughters and the other relatives in their bereavement. The funeral took place on Saturday 2 June at Duror Cemetery. There was a large and representative attendance of mourners present. The Rev. J Mackay, Church of Scotland and the Rev T.M. Murchison, Govan, conducted services at the house and grave.'

SURGERY PREMISES

The surgery premises created by Dr Grant at Craigleven in 1929 continued to operate there for many years after his demise. The medical pavilion adjoining the main house was a generous and well-proportioned consulting and dispensing suite and it served the practice purpose well. By 1991, however, the National Health Service changes taking place in the delivery of Primary Care persuaded the then doctor, Dr Macleod, that the time had come to seek new and larger premises. In what was a life-time opportunity, he seized the moment and privately purchased the local, run-down railway station, which had been closed by Dr Beeching in the 'Railway Cuts' of 1965 and set about restoring and converting it for use a modern medical centre. The project was to catch the imagination of the local people and the wider public as well. The building had not only been restored to the point of gaining a National Award – the 1993 Association for the Protection of Rural Scotland Award – it had been created, in the first place, as a tribute to the memory of Dr Lachlan Grant and in recognition of the professional service both he and his successor, Dr William MacKenzie, had provided.

The two consulting rooms within were dedicated in their names – 'The Grant Room' and 'The MacKenzie Room.' In an added tribute to Dr Lachlan Grant, Dr Macleod invited the three daughters of Dr Grant to officially open the new Medical Centre on 6 April 1992. At the well attended ceremony on the day, the blue ribbon was proudly cut, to great acclaim, by Dr Marie, who was assisted by her sister Sheena; the youngest sister Eleanora, unable to be present, was represented by Sheena's daughter, Mrs Susan MacLennan. The Ballachulish Medical Centre remains to serve the National Health Service locally and stands in shining tribute to Dr Lachlan Grant and his memory within the community of Ballachulish and Glencoe. It also serves as a reminder that throughout the years stretching from 1900 to 2003, the local community itself has been served by only three principal GPs in that 103-year period of time:

Dr Lachlan Grant   1900 to 1945
Dr William MacKenzie   1945 to 1977
Dr Roderick Macleod   1977 to 2003

In itself, this appears a pretty unique detail in the history of rural medical practice in Scotland over one century.

Medical Centre Opened
~ it's official

The official opening of the Medical Centre in Ballachulish took place in excellent weather on the 8th April, 1992.

As the large crowd of local people, friends from afar and guests gathered at the Centre, four immaculately turned out pipers from the Lochaber High School Pipe Band provided suitable stirring music for this Highland event.

SPEECH

The ceremony began precisely at 11.15am with prayer by the Rev. Robert Malloch, minister of St. Munda's Church, Glencoe. Dr. Roderick Macleod, in an opening speech, welcomed everyone, specially the Guest of Honour, Dr. Marie Grant.

He went on to thank the very many people who had contributed to the conversion of an old, decaying railway station building into a busy, modern Medical Centre.

RELAY RACE

He spoke about "setting standards, not following them"; describing the Health Service as "not being on its back, but on the march". He said that the development need not have happened. He often likened life to a relay race. We take up the baton from those who have gone before, carry it forward a little, then pass it on to someone else for the future. That's how he felt about the new Medical Centre. There's been progress; it's a reasonable facility; he is proud of what has been accomplished.

Dr. Macleod then introduced Dr. Marie Grant, who, with her two sisters, was brought up in the village. Their father, Dr. Lachlan Grant, was the local GP from 1900

- 1945 and latterly she was in practice with him.

She expressed her pleasure at being back in Ballachulish for this important occasion. After a few more words, she cut the ribbons and declared the Medical Centre officially open.

Dr. and Mrs. Macleod's two daughters presented bouquets as the doors to the Centre were opened.

CONGRATULATIONS

Also present at the proceedings was Mr. Robin Stewart, General Manager of the Highland Health Board. He congratulated Dr. MacLeod on the opening of the Centre, mentioning the high regard the Board had for him, specially his work in support of General Practitioners in the Highlands. "Dr. Beeching may have closed the Ballachulish railway station 30 years ago", he said, "but Dr. Macleod has opened it again".

Afterwards, about 100 invited guests sat down to an excellent Buffet Luncheon in the Isles of Glencoe Hotel. The hubbub of conversation and laughter indicated the high level of enjoyment. The Hotel was also the venue for a Grand Ceilidh for invited guests and for all adult patients who wished to attend later in the evening.

So ended a memorable day in the life of Dr. and Mrs. Macleod, his family, and the people of Ballachulish and the surrounding areas.

42 'Medical Centre Opened'

COMMUNITY MONUMENT

In a fitting public tribute the Ballachulish Community Council decided to hold an Open Day on Saturday 11 September 2012 to unveil the splendid slate monument commissioned in honour of its two best-remembered sons, Dr Lachlan Grant and Mr Angus Clark, and to set up a public exhibition on the village hall on 'The Life and Times of Dr Grant.' As already detailed in the narrative of this book, both men were entwined in the fascinating history of the village, the quarries and the community. Through thick or thin they stood firm, and they stood together. Moreover, the local people had backed them to the hilt in their objectives, and never counted the cost.

The magnificent monument was created by a local stonemason, the late

David Campbell. It was appropriately unveiled on the day by Professor James Hunter, the renowned historian, before a large public gathering including representatives of the Grant and Clark families.

Prior to the unveiling of the monument the gathering was treated to full informative eulogies of both local stalwarts, respectively delivered by Dr Roderick Macleod, in regard to Dr Lachlan Grant, and by Mr Duncan Clark, in regard to his illustrious father and worthy warrior, Mr Angus Clark.

Present on the day to grace the occasion and witness these events were Mrs Susan MacLennan (niece of Dr Grant), her husband Mr Hector MacLennan, their son Lorne and his wife Julia. Locally resident Grant family members were likewise there to represent their side of the family. Striking the balance, along with Mr Duncan Clark were his wife, Dr Rose Clark, and their daughter, Dr Alison, well-representing the Clark clan. It was a special and evocative day

The plaque reads:

This monument was unveiled by Professor James Hunter on 11th September 2010 and is dedicated, by the local community, to Dr Lachlan Grant and Mr Angus Clark, who were key figures in the slate quarry lock-outs of 1902 to 1905.

43 The Slate Monument at Ballachulish

44 The author, Dr Roderick Macleod, and APRS award, 1993

November 1993

From his new consulting room, Dr Roderick Macleod proudly displays the Association for the Protection of Rural Scotland Award (1993) – a motif, in bronze, of an oak leaf and its accompanying citation, which reads:

'The rehabilitation and reconstruction of the old Ballachulish railway station from a derelict building into a modern doctor's surgery is recognised as being of outstanding quality, not only in itself, but because of the effect it has had of creating a unique focus point for this old slate miners' village.

The imagination and enthusiasm that went into this creation is only equalled by the sureness of touch of the owner, Dr Roderick Macleod of East Larroch, Ballachulish, the architects Kelly Bruce Associates of Fort William and by the builders Sutherland Construction of Fort William.'

At the awards ceremony in the Signet Library in Edinburgh, Dr Macleod was accompanied by Mrs Macleod and their children, Seymour, Kirsty and Julia. By invitation, Mrs Sheena Roddan and Dr Marie Grant attended along with Mrs Susan MacLennan.

A great family day; and all in the name of Dr Lachlan Grant of Ballachulish.

which did justice to the memory of two exceptional men who were both reared in the close-knit village.

Ballachulish Community Council can reflect with pride on the tribute it paid.

APPENDIX I

Lectures, Addresses and Papers

Dr Grant was a prolific and indefatigable writer of speeches, lectures and letters. He delivered his speeches and addresses were delivered in college lecture rooms and in school and village halls. Large social functions, such as ceilidhs in cities like Glasgow, were frequent venues of presentation. Once delivered, these orations were unfailingly published in pamphlets, papers, and professional journals, and reported in the wider press. A short selection of these speeches and addresses were chosen by Dr Grant himself for publication and appear in a very attractive leather-bound volume. They read well individually and, collectively, give one an insight in to the fascinating man he was. The essays printed in this particular volume are but a fraction of his total output. The selected essays are:

1   'Life's Ideal', delivered to the Glasgow High School Gaelic Class Ceilidh in 1911.

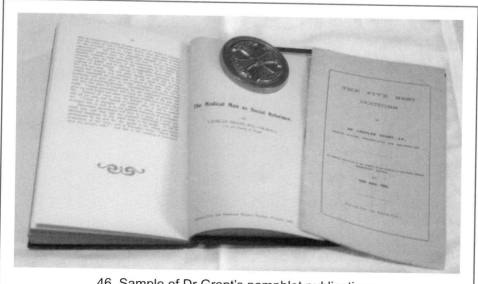

46 Sample of Dr Grant's pamphlet publications

2 'The Elements of Rational Living', a reprint of his article in the *Caledonian Medical Journal* 1912–13

3 'On Books and Reading', delivered before the Kinlochleven Literary Society in 1909.

4 'Home Sweet Home: A Health Lecture for Women and Girls', reprinted from the *Caledonian Medical Journal*

5 Aspiration: A Lecture', delivered to the Oban Mutual Improvement Society in 1907

6 'Address to The Scholars, Ballachulish Public School' on 14 July 1911

7 'Modern Highland Problems', delivered to the Glasgow High School Gaelic Class Ceilidh in 1905

8 'Mutual Aid: An Address', delivered to the Glasgow High School Gaelic Class Ceilidh in 1908.

9 'On Growing Up: An Address', delivered to the Senior Scholars of the Ballachulish Public School in 1912

10 'The Meaning of Democracy: An Address', delivered to the Oban Scots Society in 1911

11 'The Medical Man as a Social Reformer', reprinted from the *Edinburgh Medical Journal* in 1909

As already stated, it is simply not possible to list all of Dr Grant's pamphlets, publications, addresses and articles in this book. The eleven previously listed 'titles' were the only individual pamphlets that were bound together, to be published in book form. The vast majority existed as 'one off' publications.

Dr Grant's writings on medical issues, and specifically on clinical matters, formed a venerable collection as well. A sample of those titles relating to his medical compositions includes the following publications:

PAMPHLETS, PUBLICATION AND ADDRESSES by DR LACHLAN GRANT

'Micro-Organisms'. Delivered to Oban Scientific & Literary Association in the 1923–1924 session.

'Some Modern Causes of the Spread of Infectious Diseases'. Reprinted from *Medical World* in March 1929

'Infection in Wash Hand and Lavatory Basins, with Simple Method of Avoiding Same'. Reprinted from the *CMJ* in April 1930

'Suggestion in Serum Therapeutics'. Published in 1898 in the *CMJ*

'Observation on Tuberclosis and Syphilitic Diseases of the Eye'. The subject of L.G's M.D thesis, and reprinted from *The Lancet,* 15 July 1899

HOW IS THE EARLY DIAGNOSIS OF PULMONARY TUBERCULOSIS TO BE MADE?

SIR,—In your issue of November 24th Dr. A. Garvie rightly expresses the views of the profession on the difficulties of an early diagnosis of cases of pulmonary tuberculosis. He asks for the practical experiences of fellow general practitioners in connexion with the earliest diagnosis of incipient cases. In an article published in 1914[1] by Dr. Wm. Murdie and myself we pointed out that one of the chief difficulties was to ensure that patients will consult a medical practitioner at an early stage of the disease. The onset of this trouble is so insidious that, unless there is an attack of haemoptysis or pleuritic pain, it may never occur to a patient that there is anything much wrong. Coughs and colds are so prevalent in this country, especially in the winter, that, as a rule, nothing very much is thought of catarrhal attacks, and it is only when a patient begins to feel weak, loses weight, and suffers from anorexia, or one of the complications of the disease appears, that a medical man is consulted. An

[1] *Medical Press and Circular.* June 24th, 1914.

effective plan to meet this difficulty might be to distribute at intervals a short circular to every household explaining in a judicious manner the mild onset of symptoms and the harmfulness of delay in having an infection of this kind attended to. This is already done by some municipal councils in connexion with cancer. With one-fourth of our population insured, and so entitled to free medical advice, any patients in this section could be assured as to whether or not they were suffering from consumption.

The earlier the stage the easier is it to miss a definite diagnosis. The most careful percussion and auscultation may reveal little or nothing. Diagnosis by means of the *x* rays, tuberculin tests, or serum reactions, cannot be generally applied. The simplest and one of the most valuable tests at our disposal is the careful use of an accurate clinical thermometer. It is advisable to leave the thermometer in longer than usual to ensure a correct reading. When from the history and symptoms a suspicion of incipient tuberculosis arises, if an elevation of temperature occurs at some time of the day of even a half to three-quarters of a degree above the normal for some days, we hold that such a case should have the most careful observation so as to endeavour to prevent it going on to be an "open" case of pulmonary tuberculosis.

Unfortunately, many patients at the present time do not present themselves for diagnosis or treatment until they are already expectorating sputum. In such instances it is strongly advisable to have the most thorough and repeated examinations of the secretions for the tubercle bacillus. We should not be content with one or two negative results; but in all clinically suspicious cases should persevere with the search, examining the sputa at different intervals, even six, eight, or nine times, until we are fairly certain of the presence or absence of the bacillus of tubercle. Again, a complete bacteriological and cytological examination of the sputum is of great value in distinguishing between a pneumonic or influenzal infection, simple bronchial catarrh, and a tuberculous infection of the respiratory tract. This should be made at the earliest opportunity at the nearest laboratory.—I am, etc.,

Ballachulish, Nov. 26th. LACHLAN GRANT.

47 Letter to *British Medical Journal*

'Strychnine as a Factor in Causing Cerebral Haemorrhage'. Reprinted from *The Lancet*, 28 April 1900

'On Haemophilia and its Treatment'. Reprinted in the *CMJ*, April 1906

'Mental Depression'. Published in the *BMJ*, 29 March 1922

'Educating the Patient'. Reprinted from *The Practitioner* in January 1922

'Aluminium Throat Swabs' (jointly with Dr William Murdie). Reprinted in the *BMJ* 1922

'Puerperal Temperature and Their Prevention'. Delivered to the Edinburgh College of Midwives in February 1932

'Prevention of Eye Strain and Light Glare'.1934 pamphlet

'The Five Best Doctors'. Pamphlet published in June 1934

'Ten Commandments of Health'. Pamphlet published April 1935

'The Waste of Worry'. Article published in *Northern Times* in June 1943

'The Grand Ideal of Health'. Pamphlet published in 1937

'The Wooing of Morpheus'. Pamphlet published in 1936

APPENDIX II

Appointments Held by Dr Grant

Dr Grant held many professional appointments throughout his long and rewarding career, played many distinguished roles and fulfilled numerous social duties and obligations. The main ones, among the many, include the following:

Pre–1900
Assistant medical posts at Edinburgh Royal Infirmary, Edinburgh.
Assistant medical post in mental diseases at the Morningside Asylum, Edinburgh.
Assistant medical practitioner to Dr MacCalman, Oban.
Medical Officer to Gesto Hospital, Edinbane, Isle of Skye.

1900 and Post–1900
Medical officer to the Ballachulish Slate Quarry Company & quarrymen.
Medical officer for the parishes of Ballachulish, Glencoe, Duror, Kinlochleven.
Bacteriologist to Argyll County Council, including laboratory services to Lorn District and the adjacent District Committee of Inverness.
Consulting Medical Officer to British Aluminium at Kinlochleven works.
Justice of the Peace for the County of Argyll.
District Medical Officer of Health duties for the County of Argyll.

In addition to the above there were major construction projects taking shape in the district for which Dr Grant had the responsibility of providing round-the-clock medical care, and these included:

The Callander & Oban Railway spur extension; Connel to Ballachulish, in 1901/03.
The Blackwater Dam, the aluminium factory, powerhouse, pipeline, and the new village of Kinlochleven; construction in 1901/1905/1907/1910.
The new south Loch Leven road construction in 1916/23, and the daily care of P.O.W. inmates, held in camp near the Blackwater Dam over that period.
The new Glencoe Road through Glencoe in 1928/34.

APPENDIX III

Organisations Contributed to by Dr Grant

On the campaigning front Dr Grant was chairman, or an office-bearer, of all the boards and committees he founded, formed and participated in, and of the various campaigns he led. Among the many activities and organisations he contributed to were:

The Crofters' & Cottars' Association
The Dewar Committee on Health Service Provision
The Highlands & Islands Medical Services
The Sea League
The Highland Development League
The Caledonian Power Bill
The Fostering of the Gaelic language and culture
British and Scottish medical journals
Daily and weekly newspapers
Journalist to the *Daily Record*

While dealing with these matters his correspondence load must have been vast yet he still remained a prolific pamphlet writer, speechwriter and lecturer. Publication of his *New Deal for the Highlands* was, in itself, a massive administrative exercise. In parallel with all that, the charitable and fund-raising organisations, especially among the city Gaels of Glasgow, Inverness and Oban, held his constant attention and attracted his support; he was always the invited guest speaker, or the chairman of ceilidhs, and Mrs Grant, with her musical singing voice, was in constant demand to entertain at these social events. Moreover, fulfilling so many duties at such distances inevitably involved lengthy travel time, and considerable time away from home. Their ability to manage time, diaries, household and family, and their busy medical practice, must have been awesome.

Dr Grant's input to medical journals covered many fields and topics, by way of original papers, for example, on his inventions of laboratory equipment, on infection control and discussions on the research findings by colleagues. He also contributed 'Letters to the Editor' in publications ranging from the *British Medical Journal* to the *Caledonian Medical Journal* and *The Lancet*. In terms of both quantity and quality, his output makes impressive reading. To crown it all, between the years 1913-1921, he regularly switched his mode to journalism, with his column in the *Daily Record* ('By A Doctor') becoming a fixed feature. These articles were written to educate the wider public in health, hygiene and welfare matters, in ways to cope with personal issues, manage common medical complaints, control infections, deal with sanitation matters, and in hygienic food handling.

Dr LACHLAN GRANT, called and examined.

19,647. (*Chairman.*) You practise at Ballachulish, Argyllshire, and also at Kinlochleven ?—Yes.

19,648. You are a graduate of Edinburgh University ? —Yes. I am M.B.C.M. and M.D. of Edinburgh University. I also hold the Diploma of Public Health of the R.C.P.S. (Edin.) and the R.F.P.S. (Glas.), and the certificate of the Medico-Psychological Association.

19,649. How long have you been in Ballachulish ?— For ten or eleven years.

19,650. The Kinlochleven practice is a new practice ?— Yes. I am the doctor for the parish which includes Kinlochleven.

19,651. But the population has come there recently ?— Yes, within the last four and a half years.

19,652. What is the population of Kinlochleven ?— Between 1100 and 1200.

19,653. And that is all in addition to your previous practice ?—Yes, but they have a resident man besides me.

19,654. How long has that doctor been there ?—Four years.

19,655. The population over which you practise amounts to 3500 ?—Yes.

19,656. You give in your statement a list of the towns and villages along with their approximate population ?— Yes,—Ballachulish and Glencoe, 1400, Kinlochleven, 1100, Kintallen and Duror, 450, North Ballachulish and Onich, 500, and Ardgour, 200.

48 Dr Grant's Evidence to Dewar Committee (page 392)

19,657. What is the farthest that you have to go to see a patient ?—Twenty-two miles.

19,658. Is that one family or a township ?—It is down Glen Etive where there are a series of families, including two shooting lodges.

19,659. What proportion of your practice is within three miles of your house ?—You say there are about 600 within five miles. Will it be about the same within three miles ?—Yes.

19,660. Then you have about 300 at ten miles and about forty at twenty miles ?—Yes.

19,661. How do you get about the country ?—By motor car, bicycle, walking, motor boat, rowing boat, steamers and trains.

19,662. Have you much travelling to do in steamers and boats ?—Yes, a good deal.

19,663. Are there some places you cannot get to except by boat ?—Yes, there is one place.

19,664. What does your motor cost you a year to run ?—About £60.

19,665. How much is that per mile ?—I cannot say.

19,666. That £60 does not include a chauffeur ?—No.

19,667. Do you keep horses too ?—No.

19,668. Did you keep horses before you got your motor ?—Yes, one.

19,669. You do some bacteriological work ?—Yes.

19,670. Do you find that this is useful ?—Extremely useful.

19,671. Do you do it for other doctors too ?—Yes.

19,672. What about security of tenure ? Have you had any trouble with your Parish Council ?—No, none at all.

19,673. But you would approve of it ?—Yes, I would.

19,674. Do you think the parish medical officer should have the same security of tenure as the county medical officer has ?—Yes.

19,675. The county medical officer has to interfere very likely with the property of certain County Councillors, while the medical officer for the parish has not to do so ?—Of course I am local medical officer of health.

19,676. And as that have you fixity of tenure ?—No.

19,677. Do you find an increase in the number of conscientious objectors against vaccination ?—Yes, at Kinlochleven more than at Ballachulish or Glencoe.

19,678. It is really a conscientious objection, or is it merely to avoid the trouble ?—It is really to avoid the trouble of vaccinating.

19,679. We have had evidence to the effect that since it was possible to get relief, the doctors have practically no vaccination to do now ?—In my district the vaccination is much the same as usual, except at Kinlochleven.

19,680. (*Dr Mackenzie.*) Is that because of the difference of the imported population ?—Yes.

19,681. They are a different race really ?—Yes, they largely come from the south.

19,681A. Your own people fall in with it quite peaceably ?—Yes.

19,682. (*The Chairman.*) How does your club at Ballachulish work ?—It works only fairly well : it is not a great success. The workmen pay me 3¼d. per week.

19,683. Does that cover attention to themselves and their families ?—Yes. The single men pay the same thing.

19,684. That is about 14s. a year ?—15s. 2d.

19,685. That is paid by all the men, whether married or single, and it includes medical attendance on the women and children ?—Yes.

19,686. Does it include maternity ?—No.

19,687. What do you get for the maternity cases ?—A guinea as a rule.

19,688. Does it include operations and that sort of thing ?—Yes, but supposing we use a local or general anæsthetic we charge extra.

19,689. You have forty men at Kintallen ?—Yes.

19,690. How many have you at Ballachulish ?—About 200.

19,691. How do you collect the subscriptions ?—They have a secretary and treasurer who collects the money each pay. It is not deducted from their wages at the slate quarries, but it is deducted at the granite quarries.

19,692. But the money is always got ?—Not always.

19,693. (*Lady Tullibardine.*) Taking both clubs you have 240 men in them ?—Yes.

19,694. (*Chairman.*) Suppose this was a private practice and there was no club, do you think you would get less or more out of your practice there ? Does it amount to a fair remuneration for you ?—No. If it was not for my outside peractice I really could not make it up.

19,695. Do you give to these 240 men more attention than you are really paid for ?—Yes.

19,696. (*Dr Mackenzie.*) Supposing you were attending them as if they were not a club, but as private patients, do you think you would get more from them in the form of fees than you are getting now ?—I don't think I would. I am afraid I would have to sue them, and that would be *infra dig.*

19,697. (*Chairman.*) Suppose there was no club here, and you attended them, would you be able to get £180 out of them, taking the risk of bad debts and all the rest of it ?—I think I would, but they have been used with the club practice for a matter of fifty years.

19,698. What I want to get at is whether you think your income would be better or worse if they paid by fees instead of club practice ?—That is a difficult point.

19,699. Do you think you are oftener called than you would be if they had to pay a fee each time ?—No, I don't think so.

19,700. Are you called frivolously ?—Occasionally, but not very often.

19,701. Do you think they would do that whether they paid a fee or not ?—They would not be so ready to do it. Of course one goes in for a little personal admonition.

19,702. When the doctor gets to know the people it does not happen to any great extent ?—That is so.

19,703. That is your experience ?—Yes.

19,704. You suggest that with the payment by fees you have very often to modify your charge and you very often don't get it at all ?—That is so.

19,705. Are those club people all insured persons ?—Yes.

19,706. Do you think it is likely you will get £80 out of the wives and families ?—I should think so.

19,707. How many of these 240 are married ? Roughly speaking a half ?—Yes.

19,708. Why do you consider payment per visit to be preferable ?—Simply because of the check on the useless calls.

19,709. But you say that that does not amount to anything very serious with you ?—That is so.

19,710. There is this to be said, that this population is just at your door ?—No, there is Duror for example.

19,711. Are they all in the club there ?—No.

19,712. I was referring to the club ?—Kintallen is four miles from me.

19,713. You are afraid if it was a club entirely you would be called unnecessarily. As a matter of fact you have not found that to be the case ?—Not so far.

19,714. Taking it from the public health point of view, would it not be an advantage if a poor person knew he could get the doctor without running up a bill ? Would he not send oftener and earlier ?—Yes.

19,715. And it would entail a good deal of extra work on the doctor ?—Yes.

19,716. You ... t have more to do, but at the same time, the patients would get a better service and from the point of view of the public health it would be better ?—Yes.

19,717. A good deal of your practice is unremunerated ?—Yes.

19,718. That is to say, when you have a long way to go you don't get a fee adequate to pay you for your trouble and expense ?—That is so. With regard to public works, some form of contract is in force as in my own practice. The Workmen's Medical Society in my own district of Ballachulish and Glencoe arrange for all single and married men to pay 15s. 2d. per annum. To become entitled to medical benefits all workmen earning their own living must pay into the fund. Confinements and vaccinations are extra. This scale of remuneration enables the doctor to give his attention to the work, though there is, by no means, anything in the shape of a fortune in it, and were it not for the outside practice one could not " make " a living. The outside private practice from the parish centres is of a varied character. The amount of professional work varies from year to year. It is done by trap, bicycle, motor car, train, steamer, motor boat, ferry boat, when not by walking. Here, the patients, as a rule, only send for the doctor when they think the case is a serious one, or when an accident takes place. Hesitation in calling in the doctor often leads to irreparable injury and death. For instance, in two families, there were

50

48 Dr Grant's Evidence to Dewar Committee (page 393)

cases of diphtheria that turned out fatal. Had I been called in in the earliest stage of the disease the chances are that both lives would have been saved. I have never lost a case of diphtheria yet when I got in the first day and administered the antitoxine.

19,719. How far were these patients away ?—One was five miles and the other was ten.

Competition.—The parish medical officer, and the local independent medical practitioners in the more populous centres like Oban, Fort William, Kinlochleven etc., are all more or less in competition. There is consequently a large amount of overlapping in rural practice. For instance, I have considerable work at Onich and North Ballachulish, though both these places are in my colleague Dr Miller's parish. This is due to my being the nearest doctor. Parish medical officers are frequently called in by patients in adjoining parishes, so that, as things are, artificial boundaries cannot be adhered to. Yet, the result is much wasted energy, and work at very inadequate remuneration. Locomotion in the Highlands and Islands is expensive and often difficult, entailing great hardships in rough weather. Take the case of Duror and Ardgour, ten and seven miles from my centre, the cost of hires—if no steamers or trains are available— is from 9s. to 15s. per visit. On trying to make a living I find myself in competition with colleagues in town and country, including other parish medical officers ; I certainly don't enjoy any fun there may be in the scramble ; but I have no option but to follow the present economic necessity.

Adequate Equipment.—Bearing on this is the lack of equipment. Parish doctors making a bare living, having no free dwelling-house, and financially unable to equip themselves with the most modern medical and surgical appliances, patients cannot get the best treatment. I quite admit there is a continual improvement in this respect, but there is still a great deal of inefficiency from this cause.

Medicine.—Patients' friends have to come for medicines and dressings to the surgery—or they are sent by post.

Outline of my work.—Before giving an outline of the work I do in my practice, I may mention I have had the following experience. House Surgeon, Royal Infirmary, Edinburgh, Assistantship in General Practice, four and a half years Surgeon to Gesto Hospital, Isle of Skye, situated in centre of island, two days weekly free dispensaries. I did ordinary and consulting practice over island. General medical practitioner here and at Kinlochleven. Have an assistant at times, but this is expensive, an I now they are somewhat difficult to get. At present I have the following appointments :—

(1) Parish Medical Officer.
(2) Local Medical Officer of Health.
(3) Medical Officer of Fever Hospital which includes shelter for isolation and treatment of advanced phthisical cases.
(4) Medical Officer to Workmen's Medical Society.
(5) Consulting Medical Officer to British Aluminium Coy., Kinlochleven Works.
(6) Certifying Factory Surgeon.
(7) Bacteriologist to Lorn, Ardnamurchan, and Mull Districts of County Council.

In the course of daily practice I endeavour to diagnose and treat patients by the latest modern methods ; and I would consider much of my efforts wasted unless I did so. I am convinced that for many diseases *laboratory methods* are nowadays absolutely necessary as an adjunct to clinical work. Much inefficient diagnosis and treatment are due to lack of the aid this modern development in medicines can give. So I should like to emphasise that bacteriological diagnosis is an important requirement in many illnesses, and is not half taken advantage of. The District Committees of some County Councils get the diagnosis of diphtheria, consumption, and enteric fever done for the medical practitioners free. I do such for some of the Committees, and get paid at the usual rates ; but the remuneration is so small it really does not pay me, and were it not that I am deeply interested in such work I should let such be sent away to Glasgow, Edinburgh, or London. For some years now I have been issuing vaccines mostly prepared in my own laboratory with very good results.

Ophthalmic Work.—On my district, eyework I find is an important branch of practice. I went over my lists recently and found I had fitted over a thousand people with lenses during the last eight years. If I did not do this work some of these patients would require to travel to one of the ophthalmic institutions in the cities.

Recommendations.—First and foremost comes adequate remuneration ; then relief from uncertainty and useless competition, and a reasonable amount of leisure. I have given the problem considerable thought, and confess I see no adequate solution along the old lines of general practice. We require a new departure in the form of a full State medical service for our Highlands and Islands. I would tabulate the essentials of such an organised medical service as follows :—

(1) A sufficient salary increasing according to length of service and work done—also a pension system.
(2) Free house with surgery—and dispensary—if no chemist near.
(3) Periodical visits to hospitals and post-graduate classes.
(4) Provision for motor cars, motor boats, and bicycles.
(5) Consultation and assistance in serious and obscure cases.
(6) Provision for cases requiring special hospital treatment.
(7) Provision for bacteriological diagnosis.
(8) Provision for X-ray diagnosis and treatment.
(9) Provision for vaccine and other special treatments.
(10) Supply of medicine, surgical dressings and surgical appliances by the administrative authority.
(11) A committee of medical men consisting of special specialists and practitioners should act as an advisory body to the Central State Department.
(12) Some leisure and an annual holiday for the medical practitioner.
(13) Regulations of an elastic nature bearing on general, medical, and surgical duties, and equipments should be formed, and issued to the medical practitioners ; or occasional visits should be paid by all-round experienced medical commissioners to each district—something on the pattern of the Lunacy Board.

With reference to point No. (3), the district medical officer should visit some general hospital at least every two years, and a fever hospital perhaps every third or fourth year, his expenses being paid, and efficient trained substitutes provided. E.g. in a few of the larger centres a regular staff of well-paid assistant medical officers should be available as locums or assistants for special and emergency work, or extra service in case of epidemics. Special medical men should also be retained for consultative or special operative work. In my opinion, it is highly desirable to have one or even two *bacteriological* and chemical laboratories in the Highlands. Such a modern, well-equipped laboratory, situated in the centre of the Highlands, providing for diagnosis and treatment, would prove of the greatest possible benefit, and the cost would not be very great. It would also stimulate fresh interest in medical matters not only amongst the members of the medical profession, but also amongst the whole of the general public in a way which cannot be arrived at by the delegation of such special work to distant laboratories in the larger centres in the south, where of necessity the bacteriologist is out of contact with the general medical practitioner whose work it is his function to assist. It may seem rather advanced to propose to give medicine, vaccines, and appliances free, as well as medical advice, but I believe it is bound to come to that in the end. And, after all, it is only a further division of the burden of taxation among the whole people according to the ability to pay. It will always pay the county as a whole to keep each or any section of it in the highest grade of health. A medical organisation like this is really a system of police against disease, and to make it effective a similar method to the police and post office is essential. As an illustration, last year I examined some forty specimens of sputum in my district, and eight of them were found to be tubercular. Some of them were only found positive after repeated examinations and special tests. Without examination, some of the cases would have been missed and allowed to develop into more " open " cases of tuberculosis, with consequent danger to those around. I hold, therefore, that if a patient with incipient tubercular disease has been allowed to get the length of having sputum—that all doctors should send the suspicious sputas repeatedly to nearest medical laboratory—I say repeatedly, as we know it is often only after repeated examinations that we find the presence of the tubercle bacillus. Supplementary to local organisations, there could be centres easy of access for various departments of specialism, say, for eyes, ear, and throat, teeth, women's and children's diseases. At present, special centres are available for mental and infectious diseases in our asylums and fever hospitals.

A Possible Compromise.—Some system of compromise may possibly be devised so that all may pay something for attendance, with extra fees for night visits, confinements, fractures, vaccine, treatments, and operations. But, whatever plan may be adopted, I don't think the capitation system will suit the country and the outlying district of the Highlands and the Islands. The time and expense incurred in travelling to patients precludes that. And there are other considerations, such as the poverty of many of the patients. If the district medical officers were under the State, the salary hitherto paid by the Parish Councils could be utilised as a portion of the standardised remuneration under a new scheme. The minds of the officers being free from the details and anxieties of fee-collecting would be better able to concentrate on the duties of disease prevention and health betterment of the individual and the community. The question would naturally arise who was to be medically attended to and who not by the district medical officer. It would probably be found that the system should be of universal application, and any who wished extra-official attention could have it by individual payment to private practitioners. But as district officers would be confined entirely to official work, the salaries and conditions would have to be adequate and reasonable in order to attract the best talent to this branch of the medical profession.

Supplement.—Some details of my Isle of Skye experiences may be of service. I have seen

(1) Cases of women having large families who never had the skill and service of a medical man or skilled nurse.

(2) Cases where distance from nearest doctor was many miles—frequently I drove ten and twenty miles, and sometimes having to stay over a night.

(3) Cases where, after a long fatiguing journey and a difficult case, no fees were ever paid.

(4) Cases of people very poor, with little or no comforts and hygienic conditions very bad.

(5) Cases where the services of a trained nurse were essential to recovery.

My experiences would indicate that, in addition to district medical officers, some organised system of "medical patrol" at stated and regular intervals would best suit the outlying sections of our Highlands and Islands. There should also be telephonic communication direct between medical outposts and also to the base of supplies, and to the nurses' homes—so that nursing or extra-skilled assistance, and special remedies, can be had freshly prepared without any undue delay.

Nursing Service.—An efficient medical service for the Highlands and Islands necessarily carries with it an auxiliary in the form of a staff of well-trained nurses available for service anywhere. These nurses would require a special equipment of items for the sick, and perhaps little comforts for the destitute. It should be part of their duty wherever they went to teach elementary general health conditions, and even sick-room cookery. Amongst the corps of nurses should be some specially trained in midwifery (mental cases), etc., to send to cases in isolated parts (glens or island) where doctor is not easily available.

Intelligence Department.—A series of tracts or handbills should be officially prepared by the medical headquarters in plain language dealing with, the essentials of healthy living and avoidance of illness. Also, perhaps, warnings of various dangers, etc., for broadcast distribution. Each county might issue timely bulletins dealing with anything special, as well as a monthly circular, for public perusal (churches have their Records, etc.). A system of popular medical lectures might be given every year for old and young on how to try and keep well. Such should be a standing order of the new territorial medical corps. Juvenile health culture and physiology classes should be encouraged, and each district should have its first-aid or ambulance classes. In, say, two centres there ought to be a Motherhood College (instruction largely by women

graduates), where girls could obtain instruction in matters pertaining specially to their health, and in subjects necessary for mothers to know.

The Medical Man as Casual Labourer.—Some of us are frequently in the position of the casual labourer waiting for a job. It will happen there is only one job for several waiting aspirants, while not far off there will be a number of jobs and only one man available. Again, some of us are so poor, we cannot afford to let any opportunity pass for making a fee. One eye has to be kept on the patient and the other on our bread and butter. The exigencies of a lean pasture make us regretfully sparing of our science and sentiment. There is a tendency created to think meanly of, and perhaps to act meanly to, our fellow medicals, but competition, even in doing good, always does that. The casual labourer is a danger to the industrial community, and the casual competitive doctor of medicine is also a danger to the public health. In a profession demanding a large strain of altruism, a paltry commercialism is fatal to its best manifestations.

Conclusions in favour of a Complete State Service :—

(1) That the case of the Highlands and Islands requires special treatment and consideration.

(2) That medical practice as carried on in the Highlands does not give the people the benefit of those advances in medical science that they are entitled to.

(3) That medical practice as carried on at present in many Highland districts is unremunerative, and this because of the time taken in travelling to and from cases, heavy outlays for transit, cost of medicines, and no free houses (such as are provided for the clergy and head teachers).

(4) That the present moment is ripe for the inauguration of a complete State medical service.

(5) That the starting of such a service in the Highlands could be done with less opposition and much less friction than in the more densely populated parts of the country.

(6) That if the remuneration were adequate to attract skilful members of the profession, that both the doctors and the public would favour such a form of medical service.

(7) That such a service should include a fully equipped bacteriological laboratory at one or more convenient centres.

(8) That, in addition to the money received from insured people and from parish and county councils, financial assistance should be obtained from the Treasury in order to make up the allowance necessary for satisfactory medical attention for each district.

(9) That only on these lines will every individual in the Highlands receive proper medical and surgical attention ; no patient would be neglected and no serious cases jeopardised through dilatoriness in sending for the doctor because of the expense, the distance, and inconvenience.

(10) That such a State preventive system as I have briefly outlined is a "coming event" all over the country in the near future.

The motive and object of all the reforms outlined is to enable the people to be well attended to when they are sick, to live naturally, and avoid to a large extent the necessity for drugs and doctors. A sure sign of progress will be when doctors have little to do but attend to accidents and the unavoidable visitations of Nature.

19,720. In regard to your proposals, who do you propose would get the benefit of this State medical service ?—I should say all the people.

19,721. Without regard to their position or their ability to pay?—Yes. If you remunerate the local district medical officer sufficiently, he will be pleased to attend all and sundry.

19,722. The Duke of Sutherland and Mr Andrew Carnegie and all these people should get the benefit of this service ?—I suppose that would have to be.

19,723. Do you think it is a feasible proposal ?—I really do think so.

19,724. (*Dr Mackenzie.*) Your point is, that you would put general medical attendance on the same footing as attendance for public health purposes ?—Yes.

19,725. (*Chairman.*) How are these people who at present pay fees to pay for this doctor ? You will let off all those people who at present pay fees. Are you not to get anything from them ?—There will be the ordinary taxation, and if you get a grant from the Treasury they will be contributing towards it indirectly.

19,726. Is the whole cost to come from the Treasury ?—No, there will be the money from the insured people and contributions from the Parish Councils and County Councils.

19,727. Why should you take it from the Parish Council? —I get a salary from the Parish Council already.

19,728. But if you are to let off the ordinary patient from paying his doctor's fee, why should you not let off the Parish Council ?—The Parish Council taxes the people for the parish medical work.

19,729. Yes, but they don't tax them in the same proportion. We have got some parishes in the county that pay 1s. in the £ for their medical officer's fee, and others that pay less than 1d. Are you to continue that present rate, or are you to take a universal rate all over the country ?—I should say that probably it should be a universal rate for the Highlands.

19,730. Who is to control the doctor ?—That is another problem. I should say there ought to be some system of local control as well as central control—I should say perhaps the Insurance Committee—and the appointment should be sanctioned by the Local Government Board or the central advisory body.

19,731. There should be some control ?—Yes, I think I would favour that. Of course the Parish Council and the County Council have it just now.

19,732. (*Dr Mackenzie.*) You would unite all the bodies and any voluntary bodies as well ?—Yes, I think that is a feasible proposal.

19,733. There is nothing contradictory in that ?—No.

19,734. (*Chairman.*) You would give this body the absolute control of the kind of doctor that was to be set down to work a certain parish ?—You mean local bodies ?

19,735. Yes ?—Of course the regulations would be framed and the work really set agoing by the central body.

19,736. And no matter how objectionable and unsatisfactory a doctor might be or might become for a parish, you would not give any right to the locality to get rid of him ?—I should think they should have the right to petition to the central body.

19,737. (*Lady Tullibardine.*) Do you not think that there would be some fear of the average doctor not being as interested in his patients if there was a State service as he is at present ?—I am inclined to think not. I should think nowadays there is such care taken in getting the best men into the profession, examinations are so difficult, and then their testimonials would be carefully investigated by the local body, and the appointment would be supervised by the central body. If an undue number of complaints were made, then there would be room for investigation. Then the work would be supervised by a Commissioner visiting occasionally, and reports on the doctor's work could be sent on.

19,738. Do you think that that would be agreeable to the profession ?—I am inclined to think it would, in the Highlands. I think most of the doctors would rather have a salary of say £500 per annum than try and work up to £200 or £300 more—they would rather be certain of the £500.

19,739. Your great objection to the present system is its uncertainty ?—Yes.

19,740. Do you not think that if there was a certain sum guaranteed that would remove a good many of your objections to the present system ?—It would help. It would depend upon the amount of work that had to be done and the sum allotted.

19,741. Would you not see a danger of friction between your State doctors and the ordinary doctor ?—I don't think so—not any more than you would have between the present public schools and the private schools.

19,742. Private schools are usually to be found in centres. I gathered that your private practitioners would be distributed about the country and would be employed by the people who did not care to employ a State doctor ?—Yes, but ultimately they would have to fall into line.

19,743. What exactly do you mean ?—The State doctor would ultimately take over the whole of the duties.

19,744. So you would have none but State doctors ?—Ultimately.

19,745. That involves forfeiting the choice of doctors by patients ?—Not entirely.

19,746. Would you not have to give your State doctor each his own area ?—Yes, but there would be some choice of doctor to start with anyway. That would have to be so, because, as I have pointed out, some of us visit adjoining parishes.

19,747. You mean that other doctors visit the same parish ?—Yes, and other parishes.

19,748. Do you not find that people like to have a free choice of doctor ?—Yes, I am sure they do, but they really don't have it much at the present time.

19,749. Owing to the scattered nature of the population ? —Yes. Each doctor is practically in his own district at present, and the people have no choice in the selection really. I believe you would get a better set of men under this arrangement.

19,750. You do not find in this part of the country that some of the poorer people rather like to change their doctor, perhaps not always for a very good reason ?—Yes, that sometimes happens.

19,751. That would be rather difficult under your system ?—If they did wish to change there might be some arrangements. As I said, the arrangements should be of an elastic nature, providing a certain amount of freedom of choice.

19,752. Do you think that as a rule the average doctor is as interested in his club practice as he is in his ordinary practice ?—Perhaps there is a tendency to rush over the club patients—it is sort of human nature—but I don't think there is really much in that.

19,753. That is what I had in my mind. You don't think there would be a danger in that ?—I don't think so, if the work was carefully looked after and suitable records kept. I am sure it would really be a good thing, and there is a chance just now of getting such a thing set agoing. It is practically a State service just now, with the Parish Councils—I am practically a State servant.

19,754. Surely your salary is provided from the rates ? —There is a medical relief grant from the Treasury.

19,755. (*Chairman.*) Do you make a distinction between centres like Oban and centres like the Gesto Hospital ?—Yes, there is a distinction.

19,756. There is a difficulty, where there are several doctors, in how the practice is to be distributed. One doctor would be apt to be overworked, and another would not have enough to do ?—One would only have to do what he could do.

19,757. I don't see much difficulty where there is the one doctor in the one parish ?—No. You have not so very many populous centres in the Highlands to deal with.

19,758. (*Lady Tullibardine.*) But you have a good many doctors going out from centres to adjoining rural areas ?—Yes. There is a good deal of that, but still, if you had really able local practitioners and arrangements for consultations, there would not be the same necessity for that.

19,759. You would keep the town men in the town ?—Yes, I think I would. They could be available for special operative work.

19,760. Do you not think the better men would tend to flock to the towns, leaving the less able men for the country areas ?—I don't think so, if the remuneration was sufficient. There are often just as good men in the country as there are in the towns.

19,761. (*Chairman.*) It does not occur to you that we might continue to get contributions from the people for the purpose of the doctor ?—I say that some form of compromise might be arranged in that way, but I believe it would be easier to get contributions from the people if such were advised by the arrangements you are to recommend to be made just now.

19,762. I am anxious there should be a modified payment for the service they are to get, just as in the Insurance Act ?—And that would include the wives and children ?

19,763. Yes, it would need to be that in the Highlands I think ?—It would be very advisable. Of course that is practically creating a State service.

19,764. (*Dr Mackenzie.*) You say your contribution per family is really a State medical service—that is to say, it is a form of taxation, such as parochial or other rates, and it comes to the same thing as if it were rates and imperial contributions. That is what is in your mind ?—Yes.

19,765. So therefore, so far as you are concerned, it is a matter of convenience whether you would realise your service through such direct contributions from families, or whether you would just realise it as it is at present through rates and imperial contributions ?—Yes, quite.

19,766. You have read the Chancellor of the Exchequer's speech last week as given in the *British Medical Journal* and elsewhere ?—Yes.

19,767. Your scheme in reality is pretty much on the same lines as he has indicated ?—Yes.

19,768. You would consider that that fairly covers the ground ?—Yes.

19,769. (*Dr Miller.*) There is one little difficulty under the complete scheme, and it is this, that insured persons who are now obliged to pay contributions towards medical benefit ought to be relieved of the payment of such contributions ?—Yes, I think so.

19,770. So to that extent, supposing a scheme like yours were to be adopted, the Insurance Act would have to be repealed to that extent ?—To that extent, unless the local Insurance Committee had powers.

19,771. You think that something like £500 a year would be a fair basis upon which parochial medical officers would be remunerated under this scheme ? ·Yes, provided they had a house and medicines given them. With regard to the laboratory, the cost would not be very great. Probably the site would be a factor, and then there would be the buildings. These would not be very expensive. All that would be required would be two or three rooms well lighted, ventilated, and heated, and then the equipment. I would say the whole cost would be about £2000 or £3000.

19,772. (*Chairman.*) What is the advantage of having it in centres like that when you have it in Glasgow or Edinburgh ?—You want a vaccine prepared at once, and the bacteriologist and medical practitioners would be in closer touch.

19,773. (*Dr Mackenzie.*) You might explain what a vaccine is ?—Many infectious diseases, *e.g.*, common colds, are caused by micro-organisms. You get a growth of the organisms in a culture tube, and you examine this and find out what the organisms are. You rub the growth into a sterilised salt solution and sterilise this for an hour to kill them. Then you start and count them, then you inoculate so many of these organisms into the individual, and the individual's system says, "We must manufacture an antidote." The organisms are dead, but at the same time they stimulate the system, and the defensive material goes to the affected part. It is almost necessary to have vaccine treatment nowadays, and you must get the organism that is causing the disease. If you had this laboratory situated centrally, it would stimulate interest among the 200 doctors in the Highlands. The cost would not be very great.

19,774. What would be the cost of running it ?—You would have a caretaker to inoculate materials when they came in, when the doctor was not there. Probably about £700 a year and about £100 per annum for materials.

19,775. About £1000 a year would run it ?—Yes. I think myself that this is one of the most important of the medical schemes in connection with the Highlands.

48 Dr Grant's Evidence to Dewar Committee (page 397)

APPENDIX IV

Miscellaneous Notes

PATON'S JOHNSTONE MILLS: MANUFACTURING ON A MAJOR SCALE

What is now an 'A' listed building was built in 1782 by the Corse & Burns Company, as a cotton mill. It was an impressive five-storey building which was extended in 1886 to include a sixth storey and a strikingly tall tower. The mill was operated by Corse & Burns and had been in cotton production for 114 years by 1896 when William Paton Ltd. acquired it and converted the mill and plant to their own industrial use as shoelace manufacturers. In 1896 their first factory, in Clark Street, Johnstone, had been destroyed by fire. William Paton Ltd. had been established by its (then) 21-year-old founder, William Paton, at the height of the Industrial Revolution in 1840, and was to remain in Clark Street adjacent to the family home for its first 56 years of trading. With the move to the new and much larger premises, the business expanded impressively to become the largest UK manufacturer of footwear laces and insoles. Production ran at a level of about 25 million pairs of laces per year and the firm was also engaged in the manufacture of hemp rope, elastic webbing, cotton tape and leather products. It was, however, through the patenting and production of a 'plaited fabric lace' in 1896 that Patons of Johnstone Mill rode to world fame. The firm remained in Paton family hands until 1990, when it became a wholly owned subsidiary of Punch Industries (Ireland). Production and trade on the Johnstone Mill site continued until 2004, when the company moved to a new industrial estate in Linwood, Renfrewshire. Sadly, the fine building the mill once was has now been reduced to a ruin by local vandalism and arson. It serves as a reminder that nothing lasts forever. That said, the full 150-year span of Paton's business life in Johnstone is illustrious and for ninety-four of those years it was sited at this once-famous landmark by the River Cart. On the Paton family record alone, by whatever measure taken, Lachlan Grant could be justifiably proud of his antecedents: his was a supreme genetic legacy.

49 Aerial view of Paton Mills
50 Gutted by arson – the former Paton Mills

GESTO AND GESTO HOSPITAL

For many generations Captain Neil MacLeod's family leased the lands of Gesto in North West Skye from the MacLeod chiefs of Dunvegan. Neil MacLeod fell into dispute with the clan chief and had to leave Gesto in 1825. He then settled in Greshornish.

His son Kenneth was born in 1809 at Gesto. He left Skye at the age of 15 years for India and set up as a tea and indigo planter, establishing estates of his own. He made his fortune while in India. In the 1840s, and still a young man, he returned home to Skye. On his return he bought lands at Greshornish, Orbost, Edinbane and Skeabost, but Gesto he could not reclaim, on the Chief's instruction. So Kenneth MacLeod of Gesto thus became known as Kenneth MacLeod of Greshornish. He proved to be a progressive and well liked laird who, among other improvements, founded Edinbane village and provided an inn, a mill and a school.

Kenneth MacLeod died, unmarried, in 1869 at Coulmore in Ross-shire. In his will he left a legacy of £10,000 from his estate to found a hospital at Edinbane and, as stated in the will, 'for the benefit of my Countrymen the people of Skye.' Details of the endowment were not finalised until 1872 and work started on the hospital project that same year. The hospital was completed and opened in 1876 – a unit of 12 beds and the first hospital in Skye. Adjoining it was a substantial stone-built house to accommodate the doctor appointed.

The endowment provided for a full-time doctor and for hospital staff. In the 1890s the salaries paid to a doctor and a nurse were £275 and £25 per annum respectively. It was decreed that the hospital was for the benefit of all the Skye people and 'the medical man is bound to practise throughout the Isle of Skye.' The medical officer, resident in Edinbane, was to supervise the hospital and engage the necessary staff. Appointed trustees were in overall charge of affairs and managed the funding. When the National Health Service was launched in 1948 Gesto, and hospitals of its kind, transferred to the NHS and continued to operate under its aegis. The hospital became a geriatric care unit in 1960, and fulfilled that role until its closure in 2006.

Notable medical officers appointed by the Trustees to serve Gesto in its early period were: Dr Roger McNeill (1883–1890), Dr Keith N MacDonald (1890–1895) and Dr Lachlan Grant (1895–1900).

THE GOOD OLD GAME OF SHINTY

The Ballachulish Shinty Club, or Ballachulish Camanachd Club, was founded in 1893, the same year as the Camanachd Association was formed. The village and its residents, male and female, young and old, have been dedicated to the game, down the generations, ever since 1893. The team has an outstanding history and its success in its early years, from 1893 up to the outbreak of WWI, speaks volume. The Club won the Scottish Cup in 1899, 1901, 1911, and 1912 – four times in the first 20 years of its existence.

The game of shinty was played locally long before the founding of the Club and it is certain that Lachlan Grant and his siblings would have been introduced to it in childhood. Grant was the age of nine years when he came to live in the glen. In the local school playground it is certain that Gaelic and shinty were intertwined. Life in Ballachulish in those days ran very much along those lines.

When Lachlan Grant returned to his 'homeland' in 1900, to practise as a doctor, he was 29 years of age. By that time Ballachulish Shinty Club was well on its feet and about to capture the Scottish Cup for a second time. From his early days in the area, Dr Grant's name was inextricably linked with the fortunes of the club. He headed its management committee and, along with a committee of accomplished and dedicated quarrymen, played a hands–on role in the whole business of the club. There is every reason to believe that he was equally generous in his financial support of the running of the team.

An example of his involvement in shinty matters is afforded us by way of a press report which appeared in *The Oban Times* on 20 May 1922. It records in detail the business of the day:

'Mr Donald MacGregor presided over a large gathering of shinty players last Wednesday. On the recommendations of Dr Grant JP, and others, suggestions were submitted for the better organisation of the Ballachulish Shinty Club, and to this end several committees were appointed. Dr Grant announced that he would give a silver trophy for competition between local clubs to encourage the game in their midst, so as to be able to obtain the best results. Dr Grant was heartily thanked for his generous offer.'

The two world wars, 1914 and 1939, interrupted the game and curtailed the club's activities, as was the situation everywhere else, but at the end of hostilities it was back to normal business, with spirited contests on the field.

There are numerous delightful photographs of the team members taken down the years around the Jubilee Park and various locations in the village. Many prize-winning occasions are so commemorated, and much happiness, pride and confidence is portrayed on all the faces. An open air photo-shoot, taken before the 1939 War, of prize-winning Ballachulish senior and junior shinty teams, along with officials of the club, including Mr D. MacGregor, Chairman, Mr Lawrie, Captain, and Dr Lachlan Grant, Chieftain, is particu-

51 Shinty Teams (Senior
and Junior), pre 1939 War

52 Challenge Cup,
presented by Dr Grant

larly pleasing. There is chair sitting for some, for others the grassy field to squat on. There is the cloth–draped table, centrally placed and laden with silverware, as cups, shields and medals are proudly displayed. Presentations like this did wonders for local morale and village pride. The fact that photographs and news reports of the kind were circulated through the local, county, and Highland press, no doubt added to the joy.

The wealth of material Dr Grant personally collected and retained, in connection with the game, demonstrates his deep love for it and pride in the fine young men who played the sport. His devotion to the game and the local club was such that he wrote and published a specially produced pamphlet, 'The

Good Old Game of Shinty.' It was given full coverage in *The Highland News* issue of 3 July 1923. What is more, on any subject of substance, like shinty, the good Dr Grant was not the person to miss any opportunity to advance its status. As a Christmas present in 1932, he sent a caman to his good friend the Prime Minister, Ramsay MacDonald! Of course such a gesture captured the attention of more than the local press. A typical report in the newspapers read: 'Dr Grant, Ballachulish, has presented the Rt Hon James Ramsay MacDonald, the Prime Minister, with a very fine shinty from Glencoe ash grown in the centre of the MacDonald country and made by a native of Glencoe. It may be of general interest to know that the PM in his younger days used to play shinty on Wimbledon Common. He has a shinty oil painting in his own room at No. 10 Downing Street.' The gentle romantic touch therein is not lost on anybody. If the gesture itself was somewhat original, the reply from the Prime Minister could not have been kinder or more heart-felt in its tone and content. It high-lights, yet again, the genuine friendship that existed between the two men and their families. Under the Downing Street letterhead the PM responded:

'17th December 1932...thank you so much for the Glencoe Shinty. Over the picture I have of a shinty match, it will find a very appropriate place. I hope with all my heart that Mrs Grant and you and family are to have a most delightful New Year and that 1933, however gloomily it is likely to open, may have some more sunshine than the year that is now coming to an end. Both Ishbel and I were delighted to have you at No. 10 and she joins me in sending all the good wishes which are in my heart for you.

Yours always,   J. Ramsay MacDonald'

Receipt of such a fine letter among the Christmas mail of that year at Craigleven must surely have cheered the entire Grant household and also given the noble game of shinty some cracking good national publicity!

MEDICAL PRACTICE IN THE HIGHLANDS

While sorting out his grand-father's papers, Dr Michael Simpson of Golspie unearthed much interesting original material that was written by his grand-father. Like Dr Grant, Dr J.B. Simpson was an avid reader and a wonderful writer and raconteur. His reflections and recollections over his long period in general practice he regularly wrote up, to publish and share with friends and colleagues. Often, such contributions were published in medical journals, espe-cially the *Caledonian Medical Journal*. Dr Michael has passed on to me the article

After ten months in Golspie, I was offered the appointment of what was then called "Surgeon to the Ballachulish Slate Quarries," and shortly thereafter I reached Ballachulish. This district had then a population of well over two thousand souls, with its centre in the village of Ballachulish and stretching round from Appin to the edge of the Moor of Rannoch, from Onich to Kinlochleven, from Invercoe to Loch Etive—a wild and romantic country inhabited by people whose memory I shall always hold dear. Ballachulish was at that time a very busy and flourishing place ; the output of slate from the quarries was large and there was no unemployment. The workmen were a fine lot of men, good-looking and well-behaved, good slaters, good shinty players, expert boatmen in sailing their small boats with jib and lug-sail on Loch Leven, and good fishermen and poachers. They were a sporting community with a philosophy of leisure no less sporting, and this spirit they extended to their medical officer, who was encouraged in his spare time to walk and climb the high hills, sail a boat, stalk a stag if occasion offered, and shoot ptarmigan on the Glencoe tops without a game licence.

I began work in Ballachulish on 1st February, 1889, and on the early morning of 13th February I was summoned to a confinement—a shepherd's wife at Achnacon, four miles up Glencoe. The shepherd waited for me and, carrying my bag, led the way to the mouth of the glen where we turned sharp right and walked up the left bank of the River Cona. There was no road then, merely a track. It was a wild February morning and the great hills on both sides were covered with snow above the thousand feet level. I walked behind my guide in a dream which pictured the 13th of February, 1692, in the very same glen. The whole scene of the massacre seemed to be vividly presented to me. I almost imagined I heard the guns at Achnacon, and I came to myself only when the shepherd said, " Is the doctor tired ? There is the house nearby ! " And I entered the house where, nearly two hundred years before, the Macdonalds of Glencoe were brutally massacred.

I cannot remember meeting a single case of appendicitis when I was at Ballachulish, and I do not think this was due altogether to faulty diagnosis. Anyhow, if unrecognized, the disease must have been comparatively uncommon. Midwifery was my great responsibility. Calls came from Kinlochleven, then inhabited only by a few stalkers and shepherds, from King's House, Glencoe, from the Black Mount, from Glen Etive, from Duror, as well as from Ballachulish and Glencoe. The patients did well, There was practically no trouble following maternity cases; and here I may say that I have never, in all my professional life, known a midwifery case in the wilds go wrong. There seems to be a special Providence watching over these women.

Finding that walking occupied too much time, I started using a bicycle on my rounds. This was a safety bicycle with solid tyres. The children in the street greeted me with excited cries in Gaelic of " Here's the doctor on his iron horse ! " One day a bicycle appeared in the village with the first pneumatic tyres that had ever been seen. These fared badly, for our roads were covered with sharp-edged chips of slate, and pneumatic tyres were not considered a workable proposition. The autumn and winter provided days in the deer forest such as had never before been experienced by me. The stalking of hinds in the big corries between Bidean nan Beann and Buchaille Etive was arduous and exciting sport. Days in the old Royal Forest of Dalness and on the Black Mount confirmed me in my opinion that deer stalking is the sport of sports. During these happy days I made many friends among the stalkers and shepherds. They were true hillmen, spare and active, with eyes like the eagle and muscles of iron. Intelligent observers of nature, charming companions on the hill, I have had real pleasure in the companionship of those men. Most of them were worshippers of nature, with a spiritual insight which puts the flippant mental attitude of the present day to shame. Not more than a few years ago, I was stalking in Ross-shire, near the borders of Sutherland, and my companion was a dear old friend who has passed to his rest. We had finished a long day's stalking in one of the big corries and were returning home. Big Donald strode ahead of me a few paces with the rifle on his shoulder. I looked back and saw the high tops in the west behind us glowing rosy pink in the setting sun. It was a wild and precipitous rock face with a savage confusion of stone. I said (thinking of the geological formation), "There must have been an awful commotion up there, Donald, before these rocks took their present shape." Donald walked on a few paces as if he had not heard me speak, then he halted suddenly, and turned about facing me, " Yes," he said, looking up beyond me, " and all made in the space of six days, and He rested on the seventh." Donald was uplifted in spirit. I was silent.

(reproduced on the preceding pages) as being of interest since it referred to the time JBS spent in the Ballachulish practice (1892–94), and it gave a flavour of life as a rural doctor in the early twentieth century. It would have certainly painted a picture of the place that Dr Lachlan Grant would have instantly recognised.

NATIONAL LIBRARY OF SCOTLAND

An archive of material relating to Dr Lachlan Grant MD, reference ACC. 12187, consists of (1) material principally relating to slate quarries at Ballachulish, 1902–8, and (2) volumes of press cuttings and related material such as pamphlets and photographs, 1908–93.

Further Reading

JOURNALS
Dr Lachlan Grant Journals Nos. 1–14, held at the Manuscript Division, National Library of Scotland, Edinburgh (Inv. Acc. 121870

BOOKS
Go Listen to the Crofters, A.D. Cameron
Land for the People, Ewan A. Cameron
The Life and Times of Fraser Mackintosh, Crofter MP, Ewan A. Cameron
A Macbrayne Album, Alastair Deayton and Iain Quinn
Highland Heritage, Barbara Fairweather
The Callandar and Oban Railway, C.E.J. Fryer
From Croft to Factory, Mary F. Gregor, BSc, PhD and Ruth Crichton BA
Old Kilbarchan, John Hood
The Making of a Crofting Community, James Hunter
Old Glencoe and Ballachulish, Guthrie Hutton
The Birth and Death of a Highland Railway: Ballachulish Line, Duncan Kennedy
Steam in the West Highlands, Jack Kernachan (ed.)
Custom and Conflict in the 'Land of the Gael' (Ballachulish 1900–1910), Neville Kirk
The Hospitals of Skye, J.C. Leslie and S.J. Leslie
The Flag in the Wind, John M MacCormick
Highland Life and Lore, Colin Macdonald
Old Johnstone and Elderslie, Don Malcolm
Hebridean Islands, John Mercer
The Dam Builders: Power from the Glens, James Miller
History of Skye, Alexander Nicholson
The Man Who Gave Away His Island, Ray Perman
The History of St Munda Glencoe, Archie Russell (published by the author)
A Shetland Parish Doctor, H.P. Taylor
The National Mod, Frank Thompson

*Recollections – a trip down memory lane in and around Tighnabruaich with Kyles
    Elderly Forum,* Christine Thorburn (ed.)
The Easdale Doctor, Mary Withall
The Hydro Boys, Emma Wood

NEWSPAPERS AND PERIODICALS
Bulletin
Daily Record
Freeman
Glasgow Herald
Highlander
Highland News
Inverness Advertiser
Inverness Courier
Northern Chronicle
Oban Times
Ross-shire Journal
Scotsman

MEDICAL PRESS
British Medical Journal (BMJ)
Caledonian Medical Society Journal (CMJ)
The Lancet

Biographical Notes

RODERICK MACLEOD was born and brought up in Skye. A native Gaelic speaker, he was educated at Portree High School and Aberdeen University, graduating in medicine in 1970. After NHS house officer appointments in Aberdeen and Perthshire, he trained at the Royal Army Medical College, Millbank, London, and served five years as Captain in the RAMC. He served primarily as the RMO to the 1st Bn The Gordon Highlanders in Fort George, Northern Ireland and Singapore. Completing his army service as families medical officer to BOAR in Paderborn and Sennelager, and SHO in obstetrics at Colchester Military Hospital, Essex, he briefly took up post as a GP in Stirlingshire before his appointment to the single-handed medical practice at Ballachulish, Argyll in 1977.

When he retired as GP in Ballachulish in 2003, Roderick Macleod was only the third GP to hold the appointment in 103 years, Dr Lachlan Grant (1900–1945) and Dr William McKenzie (1945–1977) being his only predecessors in that span of time.

Craigleven remains the Macleod family's residence.

JAMES HUNTER CBE, FRSE is Emeritus Professor of History at the University of the Highlands and Islands (UHI) where, between 2005 and 2010, he was director of the UHI Centre for History. He is one of the vice-chairs of the Scottish Government's Land Reform Review Group. The author of 12 books on the Highlands and on the region's worldwide diaspora, James Hunter has also been active in the public life of the area. In the mid-1980s, he became the first director of the Scottish Crofters Union, now the Scottish Crofting Federation. Later he served for 6 years as Chairman of Highlands and Islands Enterprise, the north of Scotland's development agency. In the course of a varied career, James Hunter has also been an award-winning journalist. His latest book, *From the Low Tide of the Sea to the Highest Mountain Tops*, was published by the Islands Book Trust in March 2012. He is working on a further book about the Sutherland Clearances.

'Dr Lachlan Grant - The Highland Hippocrates'

Dr Lachlan Grant MB CM (with Distinction) 1894, MD (with Commendation) 1896, DPH, RCPS Ed, RFPS Glasg, 1921, JP for Argyllshire.

In 2012, the Royal College of General Practitioners in Scotland recognised the contribution Dr Lachlan Grant made to medical practice in his lifetime, and commissioned a portrait of him and his pursuits. Lochaber artist Alistair Smyth has captured this spirit in his art work. And it depicts: general practice, public health, and laboratory diagnostics; the Dewar Committee and Health Service; his patients, the local quarries, crofters, cottars, fishermen and foresters; rural transport by horse and cart; Grant's campaigning pamphlets, and his remarkable personal friendship with the Prime Minister Ramsay MacDonald.